52

VIRGINIA

weekends

52
VIRGINA
weekends

Lynn Seldon

COUNTRY ROADS PRESS
Oaks • Pennsylvania

52 Virginia Weekends

Published by Country Roads Press
P.O. Box 838, 2170 West Drive
Oaks, PA 19456

Text design by Studio 3.
Cover photograph courtesy of Virginia Division of Tourism.
    Hang gliding over Monticello, Charlottesville.
Illustrations by Dale Ingrid Swensson.
Map by Allen Crider.
Typesetting by Typeworks.

ISBN 1-56626-132-5

Library of Congress Cataloging-in-Publication Data

Seldon, W. Lynn.
    52 Virginia weekends / author, W. Lynn Seldon, Jr. ; illustrator,
    Dale Swensson.
        p.   cm.
    Includes index.
    ISBN 1-56626-132-5
    1. Virginia – Tours.   I. Title.
    F224.3.S44   1995
    917.5504′43 – dc20   95-12802
                                                                CIP

Printed in the United States of America.
10 9 8 7 6 5 4 3 2 1

*To Cele and other lovers
of weekends in Virginia*

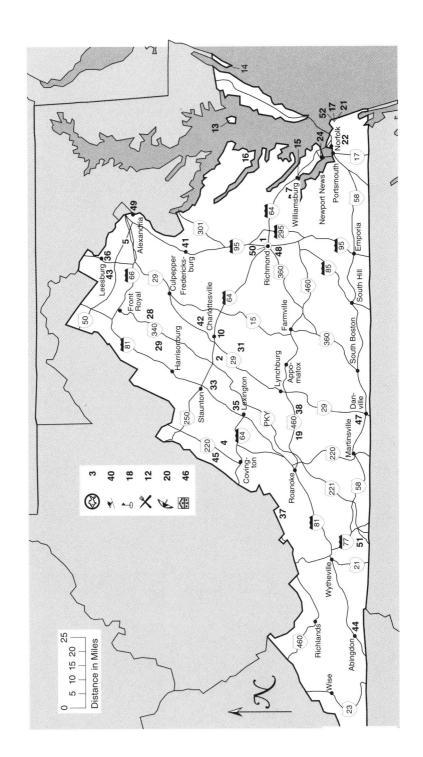

Distance in Miles

0 5 10 15 20 25

Contents

Spring

Summer

Fall

Winter

*"On the whole, I find nothing anywhere else . . .
which Virginia need envy."*

– Thomas Jefferson

Introduction

"Virginia is for Lovers" of weekends. There's a lot to love: the history, the southern charm of the people and places, the mountains, the water, the big cities, and the small towns. All of this makes for many great weekend options.

I was born and raised in Virginia and have lived in the state all my life, except for four years in the Army. My Army time gave me a wanderlust that led to a career of travel. I'm a travel writer and photographer by trade and roam the world in search of a good story. But there's nothing better than a weekend spent in Virginia.

Preparing this book renewed my immense love for everything this state has to offer the weekend traveler. My companion for every weekend and word was my soulmate and wife, Cele. We spent every possible weekend researching ideas for this book.

I've chosen a variety of weekends to expose readers to the variety of experiences the state offers, so you'll find a weekend offering almost any special experience you may be seeking.

My research and travels for this book put me in contact with some great resources that can help other Virginia-lovers. I highly recommend contacting tourism organizations for information and tips to make your own drives even more enjoyable.

The Virginia Division of Tourism (901 East Byrd Street, Richmond, VA 23219, 804-786-4484 or 800-932-5827) is an incredible resource for travel in the Old Dominion. Martha Steger and her staff were a huge help to me and are ready to help any readers of this book.

The Virginia Department of Agriculture and Consumer Services (P.O. Box 1163, Richmond, VA 23209, 804-786-0481) helps promote the state's great agricultural products and wine production. Contact them about the Virginia's

Finest program for agricultural product promotion and for information about Virginia's wines and wineries.

I highly recommend staying in the bed-and-breakfasts, small inns, and other local accommodations throughout the state. There are many excellent books about bed-and-breakfasts, as well as several organizations to help you contact them. Call 800-BNB-1293 for a free publication about Virginia's bed-and-breakfasts and country inns.

State parks systems (as well as several national parks) are located throughout the state. Virginia has actively promoted and preserved the variety of parks throughout the state and they can make ideal diversions or destinations for any weekend. For more information about the state parks, contact the Department of Conservation and Recreation at 203 Governor Street, Ste. 302, Richmond, VA 23219, 804-786-1712.

Along with the above resources, this book could not have been written without the help of many people. Everywhere we went in the state, we told people about the project, and they did their best to help make the book better for future weekend visitors.

I thank Ray Jones and Margery Read at Country Roads Press for asking me to write this book and supporting the creative process. Many of my friends in Richmond have contributed great ideas that made their way into the book. My parents and family contributed a love of their state and support of this travel-writing dream that I have somehow made a reality.

My wife, Cele, has been there for me, on the road and at the computer, for the entire project. In many ways, this book is our joint project and a gift of thanks to the state for having so many wonderful weekends to enjoy.

Spring

1 A Capital City
Richmond

Richmond is a city rich with tradition and ripe with growth. It's a great place to spend a weekend.

Richmond is at the heart of everything wonderful about the Old (and new) Dominion, offering an interesting blend of historic and modern. Over a billion dollars of shiny new buildings grace the downtown skyline, but they coexist with restored mansions, museums, and warehouses. Richmonders and visitors alike enjoy the new and old riches, but city life still moves at a southern gentleman's (and gentlewoman's) pace.

And at the center of Richmond is Court End, an eight-block section of the downtown area, which contains nine National Historic Landmarks, three museums, and eleven other buildings on the National Register of Historic Places. Its focal point is the capitol at Second and Grace Streets, the second-oldest working capitol in the United States, after Maryland's in Annapolis. The capitol was designed by Thomas Jefferson and modeled after a Roman temple in Nimes, France.

Among the other buildings of interest surrounding the capitol is the recently renovated Executive Mansion, home of the state's governor. Another is Richmond's old City Hall, on Capitol Square. Built in the Gothic Revival style, it houses the courtroom from which the area derives its name. Morton's Row along Governor Street is another highlight, lined with Italianate buildings once used as residences and now housing state offices.

Next on the Court End neighborhood tour is the John Marshall House at Ninth and Marshall Streets. This was his residence for forty-five years while he served as Secretary of State, Ambassador to France, and Chief Justice of the Supreme Court. The house showcases an interesting collection of Marshall's memorabilia, a monument to his eventful and highly successful life.

The Wickham-Valentine House on Clay Street provides a glimpse into the life of John Wickham, who built the house in 1812 when he was Richmond's wealthiest citizen. The property includes the Valentine Museum, which reveals Richmond's varied history through excellent exhibits and slides.

Nearby, on Clay Street, the White House of the Confederacy provides further insight into Richmond's Civil War role. The home served as the residence of Jefferson Davis, president of the Confederacy from 1861 to 1865. It is the centerpiece of the Museum of the Confederacy and houses the largest collection of Confederate memorabilia in the nation.

From its past role as capital of the Confederacy to its present role as capital of the Old Dominion, Court End has served as a mecca for Richmond's downtown. It's the ideal historical base for visitors.

Perhaps like no other area, however, Shockoe Slip best displays how Richmonders combine the past and present to create an enjoyable future. Shockoe Slip was a lively area full of stores and warehouses in the nineteenth century, but it fell into decay when commerce slowed along the James River.

Today, the Slip is again lively, but now it's full of diners,

The elegantly columned capitol in Richmond

shoppers, and strollers. At the head of the Slip is the sparkling Omni Richmond Hotel and the James Center, the sleek office center that exemplifies the business boom. But even here, you're just steps away from a cobblestoned walk into Richmond's past.

In many ways, the James River has dictated how Richmond developed into a business hub. Today, the biggest news along the riverfront is the recent opening of Valentine Riverside at the river's falls. This groundbreaking living history museum offers a unique experience that has locals and visitors turning out in record numbers.

The eight-acre complex is located at the restored nineteenth-century Tredegar Iron Works on the banks of the James River. An interactive history park, it boasts the museum world's most advanced technology in a historically rich setting.

All these activities are included in the admission price: raft rides on the river; two-hour bike rides along the James River Canal Walk to the Great Shiplock Park and Church Hill; guided walking tours focusing on topics such as industrial history, Belle Isle, African-American life, and the Civil War; guided motor tours that discuss such topics as the Civil War, African-American sites, and the Hollywood Cemetery; and shuttles to Shockoe Slip, Valentine Court End, and Jackson Ward.

Other elements to see and experience in the park include: Sons of Vulcan, a multimedia presentation about the history of Tredegar; the Museum Shop; the Discovery Room, offering supervised child care and children's activities; and Windows on Richmond/Reflections of a Nation, a 360-degree panorama of the city that is transformed by "time machines" and features a multiscreen audio-visual presentation that takes visitors through Richmond's history.

Among other features in the park you'll find costumed historical actors; a historic 1930s carousel; vehicles such as a real Birney streetcar, a Vulcan locomotive, and an RF&P caboose you can board; an African-American monument; an archaeological site; hands-on interactive machinery and water-oriented activities; interpretive panels; the Electric Skyline Cafe; and an amazing sound-and-light show – Valentine's signature event.

After all of this history, weekend visitors may think Richmonders live in the past, but modern Richmond is also flourishing. This modern movement, which maintains a healthy respect for the past, can best be seen in Shockoe Bottom, a historic warehouse district. The area is experiencing renewed residential and commercial growth now that a flood wall has been completed to prevent the recurrence of damaging floods.

The oldest continuously operating farmers' market in the country, at Seventeenth and Main, has drawn customers for over 200 years. The site was established as a farmers' market by the same act of legislation that made Richmond the capital of Virginia.

Providing an eerie contrast to the lively Shockoe Bottom commercial scene is the Poe Museum on Main Street, Richmond's oldest structure and now an interesting memorial to Edgar Allan Poe. The museum reveals the life and career of this strange, but very talented, author through a collection of pictures, relics, a brief slide show, and the Raven Room, containing forty-three illustrations for his poem "The Raven."

After a day touring the downtown area, it's best to branch out to see the rest of Richmond. Tourism officials have made it easy to see a variety of sights by providing a unique ride to everything of interest.

In 1887, Richmond began the nation's first trolley system.

More than 100 years later, history repeated itself when the city reinstituted trolley service. The present-day tourist vehicles have mahogany trim, leather grab straps and seats, and observation decks. On weekends, the "Cultural Link" trolley connects visitors with thirty-one of the city's most fascinating cultural and historic locations. It passes by each sight every forty-five minutes.

Many "Link" riders head first for the Science Museum of Virginia on Broad Street. Housed in the former Broad Street Railroad Station, the museum has few "Do Not Touch" signs. Instead, visitors are encouraged to touch, observe, and experience the impact of science on life. The museum is best known for UNIVERSE, one of the world's most advanced planetariums.

Nearby, the Virginia Museum of Fine Arts contains one of the finest modern art collections in the nation. After getting back on the trolley, riders can enjoy a scenic reminder of Richmond's southern heritage. Along statue-laced Monument Avenue, the trolley passes many monuments to the South, including one of Robert E. Lee astride his horse, Traveller, erected in 1890. Also along Monument Avenue are some of Richmond's most beautiful metropolitan homes, while the Fan District offers many beautifully renovated homes and excellent local restaurants.

Hollywood Cemetery, with its rolling hills and bluffs overlooking the James River and downtown, is the resting place of more than 18,000 Confederate soldiers, Confederate President Jefferson Davis, and U.S. Presidents Monroe and Tyler. It's a thought-provoking place for tourists to unwind and revel in Richmond's past.

The Jefferson Hotel (see Chapter 50) on Franklin Street is an elegant historic trolley stop where visitors can stay or just visit. Built in 1895, it's one of the oldest and grandest hotels in the South and is now beautifully renovated. It welcomes visitors and overnighters to its elaborate lobby and interesting guest rooms.

On the other side of downtown stands St. John's Episcopal Church on historic Church Hill, overlooking the city skyline. It was here, in 1775, that Patrick Henry made his famous "Give me liberty or give me death!" speech. Guided tours present the history of the church and allow visitors to stand where Patrick Henry stood, surrounded by the likes of George Washington, Thomas Jefferson, and Benjamin Harrison on that famous day. The speech is often re-created on Sundays, providing a perfect example of the old blending with the new in this capital city.

Specifically: For information about sightseeing options mentioned, contact the Richmond Convention and Visitors Bureau at 550 East Marshall Street, Richmond, VA 23219, 800-365-7272.

Accommodation recommendations include: Bensonhouse of Richmond Bed and Breakfast, 804-353-6900; the Jefferson Hotel, 804-788-8000; and Linden Row Inn, 800-348-7424.

Dining recommendations include: Joe's Inn in the Fan, 804-355-2282; Third Street Diner downtown, 804-788-4750; the Tobacco Company Restaurant in Shockoe Slip, 804-782-9555; and any of many good choices in Shockoe Bottom.

2 Wintergreen Resort Is All Green
Nellysford

Wintergreen is a four-season mountain resort development that is all green (and so is Doug Coleman). Spring blooming season is a perfect time to enjoy the Wintergreen environment that Doug Coleman loves.

Doug Coleman has been Wintergreen Resort's biologist/naturalist for the past seventeen years and has helped bring development and conservation closer together. Along with Wintergreen's environmentally sensitive developers, Coleman was responsible for the resort's winning the American Hotel and Motel's Environmental Achievement Award and the many other accolades it has received because of its successful environmental programs.

Coleman came to Wintergreen in the resort's early development stages, and he has had a big impact on its dedication to conservation. "The environment has played a role in every stage of development at Wintergreen," he proudly states.

In charge of organizing and carrying out almost every outdoor program Wintergreen offers, Coleman makes sure that each one has education and conservation as its themes. He runs at least five field trips a week in addition to children's nature camps, wildflower symposiums, and a myriad of other special educational events that attract more than 10,000 visitors annually. Coleman's relocation programs even saved more than 150,000 plants that had been slated for the dumpster when the resort was being developed. He also recently served as a consultant to the Blue Ridge Parkway and co-authored *Important Plant Habitats of the Blue Ridge Parkway*.

Of Wintergreen's 11,000 acres, 6,740 have been set aside as permanent undisturbed forest. Coleman is particularly proud of places such as the ten-acre nature preserve, which was originally supposed to be developed as twelve $40,000 homesites. He also designed a twenty-five-mile trail system that passes through wildflower gardens and geological formations around the mountain-top community. Wintergreen is situated just a mile below the Blue Ridge Parkway (see Chapter 28), one of Virginia's (and the nation's) greatest scenic drives.

New plant discoveries of national significance have been made at Wintergreen and the towering oak-hickory canopy shelters one of the most splendid displays of springtime wildflowers in the Blue Ridge Mountains. It's the perfect spot for ecotravelers in the spring or any time of year.

Along with a wildly successful annual weekend Spring Wildflower Symposium, Wintergreen hosts many summer and fall programs for outdoors lovers. In September, Wintergreen and the Virginia Museum of Natural History sponsor "Virginia's Natural History" for nature enthusiasts of all levels. At this event, Coleman and many of the state's finest field scientists discuss their most recent findings and their favorite field trips near Wintergreen. There are dozens of programs, and Wintergreen is the perfect setting.

The fall foliage season is another spectacular time for visiting Wintergreen, with many programs, hikes, and ski-lift trips available. From the Blue Ridge Parkway to the base of the mountain, the fall colors explode for all to see.

Wintergreen Resort is located in an area that geologists refer to as "Old Appalachia." This eastern deciduous forest is undergirded by geological formations that are among the oldest in North America, making it a naturally fascinating outdoor destination.

Thanks to people like Doug Coleman, Wintergreen has become established as one of the mid-Atlantic's premier four-season destinations. With golf, tennis, hiking, mountain biking, skiing, dozens of other outdoor activities, and a great variety of luxurious lodging and dining options, Wintergreen must make Mother Nature proud.

Specifically: For further information about Wintergreen's environmental programs, contact Wintergreen Resort at P.O. Box 706, Wintergreen, VA 22958, 804-325-2200.

3 Gone Fishin'

This weekend, hang out the "Gone Fishin'" sign. The Old Dominion has a fish story that seems almost beyond belief, but the angling experience is truly a tale to be told and shared with others from spring through fall.

From the Atlantic Ocean to the Chesapeake Bay to many freshwater spots throughout the state, Virginia truly has some of the best and most varied fishing opportunities for weekend anglers. More than 250 species of fish can be found in the Atlantic, the Chesapeake Bay, and in rivers, streams, and lots of smaller bodies of water all over the state. There's a fish to be caught and a weekend to be enjoyed for everyone.

The Atlantic Ocean and the Chesapeake Bay mean a salty angling adventure for Ernest Hemingway types. Like anything else in the state, Virginia's saltwater fishing excursions are unusually diverse. You can try for marlin while deep-sea fishing, fish on and around the Chesapeake Bay Bridge-Tunnel, or head into James Michener territory for the abundance of fish in the Chesapeake Bay.

The Atlantic offers a wide range of fishing outings, from big boats out on the big blue to surfcasting into the surging sea. Popular species include bluefish, tautog, sea bass, Atlantic mackerel, flounder, and much more. The deeper waters may include billfish, yellowfin tuna, dolphin, and a few surprises. The white marlin action off Virginia Beach in late summer and fall can be among the best along the East Coast.

Chesapeake Bay anglers can bring in many of the same Atlantic Ocean fish, as well as interesting catches of red drum, black drum, gray trout, speckled trout, and lots of popular "panfish" (such as spot and croaker). It's a veritable buffet of fishing options.

Weekend saltwater fishing outings are easy to arrange through any of the state's excellent outfitters. That can mean anything from half-day trips on popular headboats to multi-day charters into the Atlantic.

The state's freshwater options continue the theme of variety in fishing experiences. As with the saltwater possibilities, there are many choices of what to fish for, where to fish, and how to fish.

"Virginia offers a wide array of freshwater fishing options," says Spike Knuth, information officer for the Virginia Department of Game and Inland Fisheries. "No matter where you fish in the state, you're bound to find fish and a good time in the outdoors." His organization is a great resource for freshwater fishing information.

With so much recent media coverage, bass are probably the most sought-after fish for freshwater forays in the state. Largemouth bass can be found in most of Virginia's lakes, while other favored freshwater fish include crappies, muskies, walleyes, chain pickerel, and bluegills. The state's stream fishing for smallmouth bass, rock bass, and red breast sunfish is legendary.

Virginia is also for lovers of trout fishing. The state's Department of Game and Inland Fisheries regularly releases more than one million trout into approximately 500 miles of streams and sixteen lakes. In addition, about 2,000 miles of wild streams can offer incredible Virginia trout-fishing outings.

The state park system and many public lakes offer excellent possibilities for family fishing outings. Most have excellent facilities to accommodate an entire day of fishing fun.

With such an array of possibilities, fishing in Virginia is simply a matter of baiting a line or calling to arrange a trip. Whether you're after the big marlin or tonight's supper, there's definitely something fishy in Virginia. It's time to hang out the "Gone Fishin'" sign this weekend.

Specifically: For saltwater fishing outfitters and information, contact the Virginia Saltwater Fishing Tournament at Suite 102, Hauser Building, 968 Oriole Drive, Virginia Beach, VA 23451, 804-428-4360.

For freshwater fishing outfitters and information, contact the Virginia Department of Game and Inland Fisheries at Box 11104, 4010 West Broad Street, Richmond, VA 23230-1104, 804-257-1000.

4 Fort Lewis Lodge
Millboro

Located in Bath County in western Virginia, the Fort Lewis Lodge is a very special mountain retreat. It offers one of the state's most unique weekends in the mountains.

The richness and sheer beauty of the land led Colonel Charles Lewis to settle in the area more than two centuries ago. In 1754, he built a small stockade to protect the southern pass of Shenandoah Mountain from Indian raids. He died a hero's death in the 1774 Battle of Point Pleasant, now widely regarded as the first conflict of the American Revolution.

Lewis's vast 3,200-acre mountain farm, once known as Fort Lewis Plantation, has remained relatively unchanged in its 200-year history, but one great addition has been the Fort Lewis Lodge.

The lodge was the inspiration of John and Caryl Cowden, who dreamed of creating an inn that would provide fine accommodations for their guests, yet preserve the natural beauty of the area. In 1986, they made their dream a reality. Today, they offer dream weekends (and weekdays) to lucky guests.

Fort Lewis Lodge is a rare combination of rustic elegance and exceptional comfort. Warm and welcoming, it will delight visitors of all ages.

The large gathering room and twelve guest rooms, decorated with wildlife art and handcrafted furniture, are cozy and comfortable. Spacious decks and the "lookout" atop the lodge's renovated silo open to views of rolling green meadows and rugged cliffs that tower above the Cowpasture River.

A few steps from the lodge is the magnificently restored nineteenth-century gristmill, where guests feast on Caryl Cowden's legendary home cooking. Menus typically feature beef, lamb, fresh trout, homemade breads, and the finest local produce.

A wide variety of outdoor activities is available from spring until fall. The Cowpasture River is the Lodge's "swimming hole," with swimming, tubing, and fishing the most popular pastimes.

Nearby trails make for great hiking and views, while mountain bikers will like the logging roads. There are even underground limestone caves for spelunkers.

An unusual Fort Lewis Lodge amenity is the opportunity to camp under the stars. The lodge provides complete outfitting for an overnight stay in the wild.

The Cowdens also provide complete guide services for deer-hunting, spring and fall turkey hunts, and pheasant hunts. Whether you're an experienced hunter or a novice, they can make your expedition safe, memorable, and rewarding.

John and Caryl have fashioned a perfect Virginia weekend getaway. With rustic lodging, tasty and filling food, and stunning surroundings, the Fort Lewis Lodge lures weekend visitors from throughout the state and region.

Specifically: Contact the Fort Lewis Lodge at Millboro, VA 24460, 703-925-2314.

5 Mountain Memory Walks
The Plains

Hiking may be popular for travelers seeking adventure, but the hassles of hiking, including the logistics of sleeping, eating, and planning, aren't. That's where Mountain Memory Walks comes in, providing all of the hiking enjoyment without any of the hassles. The company has introduced hundreds of happy hikers to many Virginia trails, as well as to the state's quaint accommodations and creative cooking.

Based in The Plains, Lucy Morison's unique company offers several dozen day walks, weekends and long weekends, and inn-to-inn excursions. On all of the walks, participants only need to carry a picnic lunch, water, and a rain jacket for hassle-free hiking at its best.

The day walks (typically Sunday) appeal to beginning walkers or hikers with limited time. Destination options include the rocky outcroppings of Raven's Rock, historic Harper's Ferry, or just walks to see the wildflowers, or the scenery along many other beautiful trails in the Blue Ridge Mountains that Lucy knows so well.

The weekends and long weekends, ranging from three to five days, sport such names as Wildflower (stay at the restored Hotel Strasburg); Old Virginia (stay at the Mimslyn, a grand old Virginia inn); Bear Mountain (Virginia's Highlands and cozy cabins); Blue Ridge Waterfall (two bed and breakfasts); Mountain Top (two bed and breakfasts); and Fall Celebration. There are also excursions for Memorial Day and Columbus Day, and many other standard or extended weekend options.

The inn-to-inn excursions (usually three to four nights at two or three inns) include: Massanutten/Shenandoah (along the Shenandoah River, with stays at Hotel Strasburg, the Inn at Narrow Passage, and Widow Kip's Country Inn);

Highland/Warm Springs (Monterey's Highland Inn and the Warm Springs Inn); Plantation/Blue Ridge (Willow Grove Inn and Fountain Hall); and several other options throughout the state (as well as some in West Virginia and Maryland).

The advantage of hiking with Mountain Memory Walks is that it has already found the beautiful vistas, special wildflowers, waterfalls, and rock formations that travelers love to see. And it can tailor excursions to almost any length and pace.

Hiking groups generally range from six to fourteen people. The multi-day hikes normally begin with a wine-and-cheese reception, followed by dinner at the host inn.

After breakfast each morning, hikers review maps and trail descriptions. Treks can generally vary from four to twelve miles, with lunch somewhere along the way. Hikers sometimes walk directly from inn to inn, but they can often choose to be driven a short distance.

The Old Virginia Weekend is typical of the unique offerings of Mountain Memory Walks. Following a Friday night reception, guests stay at the Mimslyn, with its columned front porch, terrace, and boxwood gardens. On Saturday, hikers head east to the Blue Ridge Mountains and hike beside a magnificent waterfall. On Sunday, the group ventures to another ridge on the Massanutten Mountains, overlooking the Shenandoah River.

The hikes on both days start near the tops of the ridges, making this weekend an excellent choice for all abilities. The spring trip features a number of wildflower-viewing spots and the fall trip features lovely fall foliage. The price starts at $329 per person, double occupancy.

Specifically: For dates and further information about any of the hiking packages, contact Mountain Memory Walks at P.O. Box 281, The Plains, VA 22171, 703-253-9622.

6 Gardens Galore

From stately eighteenth-century plantations to stunning beachfront villas, Historic Garden Week offers a delightful sampling of the best of the old and new in Virginia.

During the week, more than 250 of the state's finest homes, gardens, and landmarks are typically open at more than thirty-five separate events across the state. Held the last full week of April, Historic Garden Week is the oldest and largest event of its kind in the nation.

Garden Week tours have been sponsored by member clubs of the Garden Club of Virginia every year since 1929, except for a brief period during World War II. The tours have benefited the restoration of the grounds and gardens of more than three dozen historic properties, including Monticello (see Chapter 10), the Woodrow Wilson Birthplace, Bacon's Castle, Montpelier, the Lee Chapel, and the University of Virginia (see Chapter 35).

City and country gardens, as well as outstanding eighteenth-, nineteenth-, and twentieth-century houses, can be found on a wide variety of tours from the Blue Ridge Mountains to the seashore. All tours feature opportunities to see exceptional antiques and artwork, interesting collections, superb flower arrangements created for each house by Garden Club members, and many exciting ideas for decorating and gardening. Attractions can range from Robert E. Lee's pastoral boyhood plantation to the modern, glass-walled residence of well-known college basketball coach Charles "Lefty" Driesell.

Cities and areas with private homes and gardens open for Historic Garden Week typically include the following: Alexandria, Ashland, Charlottesville/Albemarle County, Chatham, Danville, the Eastern Shore, Fairfax, Hampton, Harrisonburg,

Fredericksburg, Gloucester/Mathews County, James River Plantations, Leesburg, Lexington, Lynchburg, Martinsville, Norfolk, the Northern Neck area southeast of Fredericksburg, Orange, Petersburg, Portsmouth, Richmond, Roanoke, Staunton, Suffolk, Virginia Beach/Princess Anne County, Warren County, Warrenton, Williamsburg, and Winchester.

Specifically: A brochure outlining tour dates and locations is available free of charge. A 200-page guidebook with full details about all tours is usually available in March each year by sending a $2 donation for postage and handling to Historic Garden Week, 12 East Franklin Street, Richmond, VA 23219, 804-644-7776. An article highlighting wildflower gardens on the tours and near tour areas is also available from Garden Week headquarters.

Block tickets typically range from $7 to $15, with individual site admissions from $2 to $4, depending on tour locations. Tickets are available on the day of the tour at each house and garden on the program, as well as at designated local information centers. Refreshments (usually home-baked) are served on every tour. Flavorful lunches made by local church groups and others are also available.

7 Living Like a King at Kingsmill Resort
Williamsburg

Kingsmill Resort offers a perfect weekend package for anyone . . . even a king. Nestled within 2,900 pristine acres on the historic James River and conveniently situated three miles from Colonial Williamsburg, Kingsmill Resort is a great combination of unspoiled wilderness and special resort amenities. It's a sensational base for a weekend in the Historic Triangle or for a weekend getaway.

Kingsmill guests enjoy luxury in tastefully furnished villas overlooking the James River, the golf courses, the tennis complex, or the beautifully manicured grounds. Available with a guest room or one-, two-, and three-bedroom suites, each villa includes a complete kitchen and a living room, and many have fireplaces.

Weekend hackers (see Chapter 18) are big fans of Kingsmill, thanks to three championship courses. The Woods Course is Kingsmill's newest addition. Designed by popular PGA player Curtis Strange, a Virginia native, and Tom Clarke, The Woods makes Kingsmill the largest golf facility in the state. Rounding out the trio are the famed River Course, designed by Pete Dye and the Arnold Palmer/Ed Seay Plantation Course. Together, they make Kingsmill a complete golf destination. The Par 3 Bray Links course adds a nice nine-hole diversion.

Kingsmill's complimentary sports program provides guests with free use of the Bray Links golf course and free access to tennis on fifteen courts, plus racquetball, exercise classes, a fitness center, and fishing on Wareham's Pond. The Kingsmill Sports Club is one of the state's top resort fitness facilities.

There is a wide variety of dining options, all with spectacular river views. More than 600 dedicated employees exude southern hospitality to make your dining even more relaxed. Kingsmill's parent company, Anheuser-Busch, has a motto that the staff lives by: "Making friends is our business."

Specifically: Contact Kingsmill Resort at 100 Kingsmill Road, Williamsburg, VA 23185, 804-253-1703 or 800-832-5665.

8 Plantation Country

"If you haven't been to Berkeley, you haven't lived."
— Senator Charles Robb

In a distance of less than sixty miles, the road between Richmond and Williamsburg winds through more than 300 years of Virginian (and American) history. And added to the history along the route is the beauty, which makes you feel like you've taken a weekend visit to some wealthy friends at their large country estate.

Richmond and Williamsburg have long and close connections. Williamsburg was the original state capital, before Richmond took over that role. Now, nearby I-64 makes the trip a blur at 65 miles per hour, but a weekend along Route 5 allows you to linger in the present and take glimpses into the past.

Only eighteen miles and hundreds of years out of Richmond is Shirley Plantation, the first of many in the area. You reach it by taking a scenic drive along a tree-lined road. Shirley was founded in 1613, just six years after the settlers arrived in Jamestown to establish the first permanent English colony in the New World. The brick structure is one of the nation's prime examples of Queen Anne architecture.

Just down the road on the left is one of the best "non-plantation" places to stop for a few minutes or for the night. Edgewood Bed and Breakfast offers southern hospitality, antique shopping, and, of course, a bed for the night and a full breakfast in the morning. It also boasts a pool, hot tub, and gazebo.

Julian and Dot Boulware play host in this historic house, which has served as a church, post office, telephone exchange, restaurant, nursing home, and a lookout for Confederate generals. It's now enjoying its best use.

There are eight unique room options, all packed with antiques and history. Behind the main house, Prissy's Quarters is a separate retreat that's perfect for romantic couples. Dot is a fount of local lore and can arrange many unique outings for guests. Weekend drivers should make time to stop for a few minutes – or the night.

A few miles past Edgewood, you arrive at two plantations for the price of one turn. Berkeley Plantation is one of the most popular stops on State 5, but less-visited Westover's nearby grounds feature a great stroll through history along the James.

The historic mansion of Berkeley was built in 1726 (the initials of the builder, Benjamin Harrison IV, and his wife Anne are on a datestone over a side door) and has since played host to George Washington, the succeeding nine presidents, and thousands of plantation-loving tourists.

By taking the other fork along the road to Berkeley, plantation-lovers in the know head to Westover Plantation. This home, built in about 1730 by William Byrd II, only opens its grounds for touring (you can't go inside), but it's definitely worth the drive and the walk.

Back on State 5 for a minute or so, look for the turn to Westover Church. The original church was built nearby in 1613, but the church was moved to this "new" site and building in 1730. If you're enjoying State 5 on a Sunday, try to time a visit for services at 11:00 A.M. This is a true country church.

Even if you've seen enough plantations, take the road up to Evelynton. It's worth the drive to visit the wonderful gift shop and greenhouse. Originally part of William Byrd's

*The original Thanksgiving took place
in 1619 on the site where Berkeley was built*

Westover Plantation (he named it for his daughter Evelyn), it
has been in the Ruffin family since 1847.

Time your weekend of driving so you end up at Indian
Fields Tavern when you're hungry. Just three miles east of
Evelynton, this restored farmhouse is gaining national recog-
nition for creative southern hospitality and fare.

Try to sample their peanut soup, some Smithfield ham,

the homemade Sally Lunn bread, and one of their homemade desserts. The restaurant is open for lunch and dinner and is run by Archer Ruffin of the Ruffin family of plantation fame. Just ten minutes further you can stop for the night at North Bend Plantation bed and breakfast. George and Ridgely Copland restored this lovely Greek Revival house in 1984. Highlights of any visit include browsing through an incredible collection of old and rare books, admiring the antiques (including a desk of General Sheridan's), and reveling in a full country breakfast with mouth-watering homemade waffles.

The final plantation along this stretch of State 5 is Sherwood Forest Plantation, and it's an interesting one. Sherwood Forest was the home of President John Tyler and, at 300 feet long, is considered the longest frame house in America. It has been a working plantation for more than 240 years and is still occupied by members of the Tyler family. Check out the pet graveyard and the names of past Tyler family pets.

A few miles after Sherwood Forest, civilization and the twentieth century loom ahead. State 5 heads into Williamsburg and all the historic options it offers. Stop by the College of William and Mary (see Chapter 34) or head to any point of the Historic Triangle (see Chapter 15). The weekend drive officially ends at Merchant's Square in Colonial Williamsburg, where you'll find some great shopping and incredible meals at The Trellis.

Specifically: For further information, contact: Shirley Plantation, 800-232-1613; Edgewood Bed and Breakfast, 804-829-2962; Berkeley Plantation, 804-829-6018; Westover Plantation, 804-829-2882; Evelynton, 800-473-5075; Indian Fields Tavern, 804-829-5004; North End Plantation bed and breakfast, 804-829-5176; Sherwood Forest Plantation, 804-829-5377; and The Trellis, 804-229-8610.

9 Shop 'til You Drop

Outlet shopping is quickly climbing the consumer popularity list for weekend activities, especially when these economic times mandate getting the biggest bang for your buck. With bargain buying becoming the quickest way to ease the cost of living, outlet shops and off-price regional malls in Virginia are a weekend shopper's gold mine.

All across the state, bargain-based retail stores are cropping up, and consumers are lured by the emporiums of quality merchandise. Virginia's unique buying markets are conveniently located near major highways connecting the areas of the state, Maryland, the Carolinas, and Washington, D.C.

Perhaps the oldest and most famous outlet destination in Virginia is the Williamsburg Pottery Factory, located just off I-64 at Lightfoot on US 60. This outlet is one of the largest family-owned businesses in the country, with 1.5 million square feet of space and more than 60,000 items for sale, much more than simple pottery. Because of its huge success, many other shopping outlets have grown around the Pottery (Berkeley Commons Outlet Center and Williamsburg Outlet Mall), making the area a hub for bargains.

Potomac Mills Outlet Mall, just twelve miles south of Washington, D.C. on I-95 at Woodbridge, promises factory-outlet pricing without the warehouse atmosphere. This rapidly expanding mall is among the largest super-regional specialty malls in the country, with 1.3 million square feet of space housing more than 185 merchants.

Eighteenth-century style characterizes the Waynesboro Village Factory Outlets, a much newer attraction, located off I-64 (Exit 17/94) for easy access. The mall contains about thirty-five stores within its cluster of seventeen buildings.

Weekend visitors can also take time out to visit the Virginia Museum of American Frontier Culture and the famous P. Buckley Moss Museum, just five miles away.

In central Virginia, the Massaponax Outlet Center, just outside Fredericksburg off I-95 at Massaponax Exit 44, features more than twenty-five stores carrying a wide variety of items from name brands to carved decoys.

In Tidewater's Virginia Beach area, the Great American Outlet Mall on Independence Boulevard boasts thirty stores selling such items as shoes, sunglasses, clothing, brass, and cosmetics. It's a great place to find designer labels at bargain prices.

Western Virginia offers several shopping possibilities along the interstate, including Factory Merchants Outlet Mall, located just north of Wytheville at I-77 and I-81. It's a convenient place to stop and shop during a weekend outing.

Few states can compare with Virginia's offerings of premier historical, recreational, and scenic attractions, located within such easy access to accommodations, dining, and the major outlet shopping centers. It makes any weekend perfect for shopping 'til you drop.

Specifically: Contact Williamsburg Pottery Factory at 804-564-3326, Berkeley Commons Outlet Center at 800-969-3767, Williamsburg Outlet Mall at 804-565-3378, Potomac Mills Outlet Mall at 800-VA MILLS, Waynesboro Village Factory Outlets at 703-942-2320, Virginia Museum of American Frontier Culture at 703-332-7850, P. Buckley Moss Museum at 703-949-6473, Massaponax Outlet Center at 703-373-8853, Great American Outlet Mall at 804-463-8665, and Factory Merchants Outlet Mall at 703-637-6214.

10 Jefferson's Monticello
Charlottesville

"I think this is the most extraordinary collection of talent,
of human knowledge, that has ever been gathered
together at the White House, with the possible exception
of when Thomas Jefferson dined alone."
— President John F. Kennedy
(at a Nobel Prize–winners' dinner)

Born in 1743, Thomas Jefferson – third president of the United States, author of the Declaration of Independence, governor of Virginia, and founder of the University of Virginia – voiced the aspirations of a new America as no other individual of his era. As public official, historian, philosopher, and plantation owner, he served his country for more than five decades.

Jefferson designed and built his mountaintop home, Monticello (Italian for "little mountain"), between 1768 and 1809. He saw to it that Monticello was unlike any other American house of his day. It is truly one of the nation's architectural masterpieces and is the only American home ever named to UNESCO's World Heritage List (along with such international treasures as the Taj Mahal, the pyramids of Egypt, Versailles, and the Great Wall of China).

Monticello draws visitors from around the world. The neoclassical style is highlighted by the dramatic dome, which appears on the back of the U.S. nickel. A tour of the house and grounds reveals many unique facts about Jefferson, his house, and much state and American history.

Along with rich architectural detail throughout, Monticello is filled with a variety of technological devices, many of which were inspired by mechanisms Jefferson saw during his extensive world travels. These include: a seven-day clock (indicating the day and hour), a folding ladder, single-acting double doors in the parlor, and unique dumbwaiters in the dining room.

The grounds are as fascinating as the interior. The Jefferson-designed landscape is completely re-created, including ornamental flower gardens near the house, fruit orchards, and a 1,000-foot-long garden where Jefferson experimented with hundreds of varieties of vegetables. Interesting outbuildings along the main plantation street, Mulberry Row, include dwellings for free workers and slaves; shops for blacksmithing, nail-making, and weaving; a dairy; and a smokehouse.

Monticello lies along the Constitution Route. This historic road was established in 1975 to recognize its historic significance. Four presidents (Jefferson, Madison, Monroe, and Taylor) and eleven Virginia governors were either born or built their estates along the route.

James Monroe's home, Ash Lawn/Highland, is just two miles from Monticello. The fifth president was a great friend of Jefferson's, who designed the house. James Madison, the nation's fourth president, lived at Montpelier, near Orange (Jefferson spent the night there on his inaugural journey).

Modern-day Monticello visitors will also want to visit the Thomas Jefferson visitors center for an in-depth look at the man and his house through the permanent exhibition, "Thomas Jefferson at Monticello." The staff can also provide additional information about the area.

For lodging in keeping with the area, contact the Inn at Monticello. Modern possibilities in Charlottesville include the Omni, the Boar's Head Inn and Sports Club (see Chapter 42), or the quaint 200 South Street Inn.

For dining in keeping with the area, head for Historic Michie Tavern on the road to Monticello. The tavern was originally built as a stagecoach stop in 1784. Today, the Michie Tavern complex still offers travelers great food and exploration opportunities. The focus of any visit is "The Ordinary." This unique colonial buffet dining experience offers typical dishes such as fried chicken, black-eyed peas, stewed tomatoes, cole slaw, potato salad, green bean salad, Tavern beets, homemade biscuits, cornbread, their special apple cobbler, and Virginia wines and ales to slake your thirst. The Tavern serves meals seven days a week, but only from 11:30 A.M. to 3:00 P.M.

The grounds will add to your enjoyment of the historic meal. The Tavern Museum offers tours of the eighteenth-century inn, including the Ballroom, "Private Quarters," Keeping Hall, Ladies and Gentlemen's Parlor, and the Tavern's outbuildings.

Other excellent Charlottesville dining options include: Blue Ridge Brewing Company, the Coffee Exchange, Tastings, and many casual restaurants catering to college students. Wine lovers (see Chapter 32) will love a visit to one of many wineries in the area, including Simeon Vineyards or Montdomaine Cellars, both near Monticello.

You don't have to a political bigwig to visit Monticello and the other political history prizes around Charlottesville. "Jefferson expressed the American idea: political and social pluralism; government of limited, delegated, and enumerated powers; and the fecundity of freedom," says political commentator George F. Will. "He expressed it not only in stirring cadences, but also in the way he lived, as statesman, scientist, architect, and educator."

Thomas Jefferson died on July 4, 1826, on the fiftieth anniversary of the signing of the Declaration of Independence. His deathbed is still in Monticello and his grave is in the family cemetery below the house. He was eighty-three years old, the holder of large debts, but according to all evidence, a very optimistic man.

Specifically: Monticello is located on State 53, three miles southeast of Charlottesville off State 20. It is open daily except Christmas from 8:00 A.M. to 5:00 P.M. Winter hours are 9:00 A.M. to 4:30 P.M., from November 1 to February 28. For further information, contact the Thomas Jefferson Memorial Foundation, Monticello, P.O. Box 316, Charlottesville, VA 22902, 804-295-8181.

For history-laden lodging, contact the Inn at Monticello, 804-979-3593. Modern possibilities include: the Omni, 804-971-5500 or 800-THE-OMNI; the Boar's Head Inn and Sports Club (see Chapter 42), 804-296-2181 or 800-476-1988; or the 200 South Street Inn, 804-979-0200.

For historic dining, try the Historic Michie Tavern, 804-977-1234. Other excellent Charlottesville dining options include: Blue Ridge Brewing Company (see Chapter 11), 804-977-0017; the Coffee Exchange, 804-295-0975; Tastings, 804-293-3663; and many casual restaurants catering to college students. Wine lovers (see Chapter 32) will enjoy Simeon Vineyards, 804-977-0800, or Montdomaine Cellars, 804-971-8947.

11 Three Cheers for Virginia Beers

There's nothing better on a warm spring day than a cold beer. Like many states in the nation, Virginia has become a hotbed for brewing beers and for popular pubs that serve state-brewed beers and other high-quality beer from around the world.

The microbrewery industry in Virginia is booming. Several local breweries have gained national attention and a dedicated following in the state, and they also offer fascinating tours and excellent beers. Brewpubs and other bars are also great ways to enjoy Virginia beers.

Up in northern Virginia, the Old Dominion Brewing Company was the first Washington-area microbrewery and has grown into a top regional brewer. President Jerry Bailey often gives the popular weekend tours. Located near Dulles Airport, the brewery's Dominon Lager provides a tasty introduction to the best of Virginia beers.

Potomac River Brewing Company in Chantilly specializes in ales and features Patowmack Ale, an American-style pale ale. President Jerry Russell also offers excellent tours.

Bardo Rodeo is another northern Virginia beer mecca. This huge brewpub is one of the largest in the nation, with a seating capacity of almost 900. Bardo's Bill Stewart offers more than thirty-five beers on tap, thirteen Bardo brews, and hundreds of other choices. It's a beer bonanza.

Down in Richmond, the beer scene is also being cheered by the locals. Richmond's first brewpub, Richbrau Brewery, produces a tasty range of ales in its historic Shockoe Slip location. David Magill, the general manager, plays host in Richbrau's pub-like atmosphere.

Richmond-area restaurant diners have also enjoyed the widespread availability of the brews from Legend Brewing

Company. Along with offering a small taproom and restaurant, president Thomas East Martin has made Legend's pilsner, lager, brown ale, and porter popular choices around the capitol.

The Commercial Taphouse and Grill is another excellent option in Richmond. With a wide range of beers on tap and by the bottle, this beer haven in the historic Fan District also offers fine dining.

In Charlottesville, Blue Ridge Brewing Company was Virginia's first brewpub. The bar and restaurant offers lagers, stout, ale, and weitzen to college students and students of beer.

For a look at a completely different side of the beer industry, head to the Anheuser-Busch Brewery Tour at Busch Gardens in Williamsburg. The interesting tour showcases Anheuser-Busch's time-honored brewing process and includes complimentary samples for a finale.

From small to large, many people are cheering for Virginia beers. No matter where you go in Virginia on a weekend, this beer's for you.

Specifically: For tours and information about hours of operation, contact: Old Dominion Brewing Company, 703-689-1225; Potomac River Brewing Company, 703-631-5430; Bardo Rodeo, 703-527-1852; Richbrau Brewery, 804-644-3018; Legend Brewing Company, 804-232-8871; Commercial Taphouse and Grill, 804-359-6544; Blue Ridge Brewing Company, 804-977-0017; and the Anheuser-Busch Brewery Tour, 804-253-3039.

12 Bon Appetit!

In its earliest days, weekend travelers praised the quality and quantity of Virginia food and drink. Little has changed. The Old Dominion has retained its rich culinary heritage while continuing to broaden and refine its bountiful foods.

Virginia's outstanding country hams and plump peanuts are world-renowned, but statewide food festivals reveal the true scope of Virginia fare. Events honoring apples, oysters, mushrooms, and garlic show the range of Virginia's current cuisine. These festivals and foods make for fun-filled and food-filled Virginia weekends.

Stretching between the Chesapeake Bay and the Atlantic Ocean, the Eastern Shore peninsula, with its windswept barrier islands, is home to a variety of succulent seafoods. You'll find great seafood restaurants almost everywhere along the Eastern Shore.

At the northern end of the peninsula, the quaint fishing village of Chincoteague – made famous by Marguerite Henry's book, *Misty of Chincoteague* – draws thousands of visitors each July for the wild pony round-up (see Chapter 14). Lovers of good seafood will find visits there worthwhile at any time, especially because of Chincoteague's tasty oysters and clams. Fishing boats dock daily, bringing in fresh catches from surrounding waters. Oyster and clam fans will find them served raw, steamed, fried, and many other creative ways.

Another notable seafood town to the south is Wachapreague, which bills itself as the flounder capital of the world. Nearly two dozen commercial fishing boats leave this small town's docks daily in search of the famous flat fish.

The Eastern Shore's seafood takes in a wider variety of cuisine than just oysters, clams, and flounder. Crab is an

Eastern Shore delicacy as well, with lumps of the sweet meat picked directly from the shell or patted into crab cakes and browned in butter.

Another Eastern Shore favorite is soft-shell crab. Chefs lightly batter and fry blue crabs that have shed their hard outer shells, and the result is captivating dishes.

Whatever seafood most appeals to your tastes, the Eastern Shore is bound to have it and may even have a festival for it. Some of these festivals include the Annual Seafood Festival in Chincoteague in May, the Onancock Harbor Fest in July, the Harvest Festival at Kiptopeke in October, and the Annual Chincoteague Oyster Festival, also in October.

The coastal area known as Hampton Roads/Tidewater is also well-known for seafood. It plays host to the widely known and attended Urbanna Oyster Festival each November. In addition, the area is home to two of the most tradition-bound foods in the state: ham and peanuts.

Since the seventeenth century, when settlers learned the Indian art of smoking meats, Virginia country hams have had an international reputation. Most famous are the Smithfield hams which, by law, must be cured within Smithfield's town limits.

The Tidewater area's plentiful peanut fields make this area equally well-known for peanuts. Handsome Virginia-type peanuts are the largest of the four peanut types grown in the U.S. One country restaurant, the Virginia Diner in Wakefield, is famous for the peanuts it packages. Emporia hosts a peanut festival in November, and to the north, in Surry, the Surry House is known for that most savory of Virginia soups made from peanuts.

When weekend travelers seek comfort, they often go in search of comfort foods. Brunswick County, located in south-central Virginia, is the documented birthplace of the hearty meat-and-vegetable Brunswick stew that has long warmed the hearts (and stomachs) of weary travelers. The South's classic foods of fried chicken and black-eyed peas have been familiar staples in the heart of central Virginia. Historic Michie Tavern (see Chapter 10), just outside Charlottesville, serves this type of fare, with lots of cornbread, biscuits, and coleslaw.

Perched on a nearby mountaintop is the home of Thomas Jefferson, Monticello (see Chapter 10). Jefferson's enlightened approach to eating and drinking molded the course of Virginia's food and wine history.

In addition to framing the nation's Declaration of Independence and designing works of architecture, Jefferson was deeply interested in food. To his gardens at Monticello, Jefferson brought sophisticated vegetables and plants from Europe to grow for his own table, including Belgian endive, eggplant, artichokes, and salsify. He was also one of the state's original vintners.

Mark Langenfeld, chef of Lemaire restaurant in the Jefferson Hotel in Richmond (see Chapter 50), has studied the culinary writings of Jefferson and turned his research into recipes. In developing a style of Southern haute cuisine, he stuffs roast pheasant with oysters and Virginia ham or fills chicken breasts with Virginia apples and crushed peanuts.

One central Virginia festival that incorporates the best of the Virginia food and wine world is the Monticello Wine and Food Festival and Bacchanalian Feast in October at the Boar's Head Inn (see Chapter 42) in Charlottesville.

For garlic-lovers, the Virginia Garlic Festival Association in Amherst provides a "stinking good time" each fall. Garlic specialties and events are combined with music and wine tastings for an unusual weekend festival.

From ginger-scented, horseshoe-shaped shortbread to award-winning applewood-smoked trout, northern Virginia is home to many specialty food products. A constant demand from nearby Washington, D.C., for gourmet products and up-scale produce, including culinary herbs and shiitake mush-rooms, helps the area's food industry to thrive.

Won Shan Mushroom Farm in Catlett is one of several farms that grow the meaty, earthy mushrooms that are sautéed in fine restaurants in Washington, D.C., throughout Virginia, and elsewhere. An annual mushroom festival in Front Royal combines mushrooms and Virginia wines for a epicurean event.

Northern Virginia, like several other areas in the state, is known for its vineyards and wineries. The state's wine indus-try now includes more than forty wineries, and has ripened in recent years and gained the respect of wine critics at home and abroad (see Chapter 32). Native son Thomas Jefferson, who was the first to recognize that the state's climate was suitable for premium grapes, would have been proud. Vine-yards in northern Virginia include Piedmont, Willowcroft, Linden, Loudoun Valley, and Swedenbourg.

In the west, the fertile valley called Shenandoah yields an abundance of fruits and vegetables that give Virginia cuisine diversity. It also hosts an array of events, from the Shenan-doah Apple Blossom Festival in Winchester in the spring to the harvest festivals throughout the valley in the fall.

Virginia is one of the nation's top six apple producers. Red and Golden Delicious, Rome, Stayman, York, Winesap, Granny Smith, Jonathan, and Gala are a few of the varieties found in the hillside groves at the northern tip of the Shenan-doah Valley. This wealth is the reason that Winchester, the state's top apple-packaging location, calls itself the apple capital of the world.

Numerous harvest festivals celebrate the apple crop in the valley's tree-covered hills. One, the Annual Apple Harvest Arts and Crafts Festival in Madison Heights, features homemade Brunswick stew along with apple pies, apple puffs, and apple butter.

The rich soil of the Shenandoah Valley also nurtures sweet peaches, nectarines, and many other food crops. Another specialty food product from this area is the valley's flavorful tomato, which is sun-ripened, dried, and sold to gourmet stores around the world.

Poultry is raised in abundance as well. Broiler chickens are the second-largest agricultural product for the state. The recognized birthplace of the commercial turkey industry, Rockingham County proudly calls itself the turkey capital of the world.

Several farms in the region–Hemlock Spring, Ingleside, Orndorff's, and Shenandoah Fisheries–farm the rainbow trout found on many menus. When you're dining in the Shenandoah Valley, be sure to try the trout when it's featured.

Route 11 Potato Chips, just a block off US 11 in Middletown, features a unique Virginia food item. Housed in Middletown's old Feed Store, Chris Miller has created a mecca for potato chip lovers.

You can watch as the master chipman makes the freshest and tastiest potato chips imaginable. Some unique options include seasonal Yukon Gold potato chips, Purple Peruvian chips, sweet-potato chips, and mixed root-vegetable chips (made of taro root, beets, parsnips, and carrots).

The store offers eleven-ounce "personal munch" bags; one-and-one-half-pound "gift-giving" tins; and three-pound "let's party" bags. Chris offers shipping for phone or fax orders, but be sure to stop by for a visit and snack.

The beauty of the southwest Blue Ridge Highlands attracted settlers who didn't mind rugged living. Some of the hearty mountain fare that fueled pioneer activities included cornbread and beans, venison, wild turkey, and pumpkins.

In the gardens of the Historic Crab Orchard Museum and Pioneer Park grows a particular green bean with a history of its own. The Witten bean was cultivated in the 1830s by the first permanent settlers of the same name that lived in the Tazewell area. It is said that the Wittens were trading the tasty beans in the surrounding areas before the Civil War.

Cuisine in this part of the state has grown beyond its rustic roots. At Chateau Morrisette Winery and Restaurant at the Meadows of Dan, visitors can dine on foods that represent the most recent culinary trends, including roast lamb loin in Southwestern black bean sauce with jalapeño corn pudding, guacamole, and roasted yellow pepper aioli. The winery is also making a name for itself because of its numerous music festivals, held from May to October.

Sheep are raised in southwest Virginia's cool mountain climate, as are beef and dairy cattle. In fact, the Virginia Cattle Industry Board and the Virginia Sheep Federation are both headquartered in the southwest Blue Ridge Highlands.

Whatever the season or weekend, Virginia's mountain empire celebrates with festivals, such as Wytheville's Wine and Cheese Festival in May, Christianburg's New River Valley Herb Festival in August, Radford's Septemberfest, and Rich Creek's Ox Roast and Autumnfest in September.

Whether weekend diners favor the hearty foods of the southwest Blue Ridge Highlands and the Shenandoah Valley, the Southern cuisine of central Virginia, the epicurean tastes of northern Virginia, or the seafood of the Eastern Shore and Tidewater/Hampton Roads area, everyone agrees that Virginia is for food lovers.

Specifically: On the Eastern Shore, contact: the Harvest Festival at Kiptopeke at 804-787-2460; the Annual Chincoteague Oyster Festival at 804-336-6161; the Annual Seafood Festival in Chincoteague at 804-787-2460; and the Onancock Harbor Fest at 804-787-3363. For general information, write or call the Eastern Shore Tourism Commission, P.O. Box R, Melfa, VA 23410, 804-787-2460 and the Chincoteague Chamber of Commerce, P.O. Box 258, Chincoteague, VA 23336, 804-336-6161.

In Hampton Roads/Tidewater, contact: the Urbanna Oyster Festival at 804-758-0368; the Isle of Wight visitors center at 130 Main Street, Smithfield, VA 23430, 804-357-5182 or 800-365-9339; and the Virginia Diner at 804-899-3106.

In central Virginia, contact: the Monticello Wine and Food Festival and Bacchanalian Feast in Charlottesville at 804-296-4188; the Charlottesville/Albemarle Convention and Visitors Bureau at P.O. Box 161, Charlottesville, VA 22902, 804-977-1783; Historic Michie Tavern at 804-977-1234; Monticello at 804-295-8181; and the Jefferson Hotel at 804-788-8000.

In northern Virginia, contact: the Annual Virginia Mushroom Festival in Front Royal at 800-338-2576, the Appalachian Mushroom Growers Association at 703-923-4774, Won Shan Mushroom Farm at 703-788-1127, Piedmont Vineyards and Winery at 703-687-5528, Willowcroft Farm Vineyards at 703-777-8161, Linden Vineyards at 703-364-1997, Loudoun Valley Vineyards at 703-882-3375, and Swedenbourg Estate Vineyard at 703-687-5219.

In the Shenandoah Valley, contact: the Shenandoah Apple Blossom Festival in Winchester at 800-662-1360, the Winchester Chamber of Commerce, at 703-662-4135 or 800-662-1360, Hemlock Springs Trout Farm at 703-867-5659,

Ingleside Trout Farm at 703-463-9760, Orndorff's Rainbow Trout Farm at 703-436-3384, Shenandoah Fisheries at 703-433-2395, and Route 11 Potato Chips at 703-869-0104.

In the southwest Blue Ridge Highlands, contact: Septemberfest in Radford at 703-639-2202, the Ox Roast and Autumnfest in Rich Creek at 703-726-2261, the Wine and Cheese Festival in Wytheville at 703-228-3211, the New River Valley Herb Festival in Christiansburg at 703-382-2653, the Historic Crab Orchard Museum and Pioneer Park at 703-988-6755, Chateau Morrisette Winery and Restaurant at 703-593-2865, the Virginia Cattle Industry Board in Daleville at 703-992-1009, and the Virginia Sheep Federation in Blacksburg at 703-231-9159.

13 Tangier Island

Tangier Island is, quite simply, one of Virginia's most unique destinations. This remote island haven in the middle of the Chesapeake Bay makes for an unusual, yet ideal, weekend outing from the spring to the fall.

Discovered by Captain John Smith in 1608, Tangier Island is still being discovered by adventurous travelers today. Getting there is definitely half the fun.

There are several ways to get to Tangier Island by boat, and the trip takes less than one and a half hours. On the western shore of the Chesapeake Bay, the Tangier Island Cruises' *Captain Thomas* provides daily service to and from Reedville (generally from May to September). The same friendly family runs Tangier Island Cruises' *Steven Thomas* out of Crisfield, Maryland, on the Eastern Shore, with trips available from the spring until the fall.

Seasonal service is also offered by Tangier Mail and Freight Service out of Onancock, Virginia, on the Eastern Shore. You buy your ticket at the historic Hopkins and Bro. Store, one of the oldest general stores on the East Coast. One final option is to take the U.S. mailboat *Doralena,* which runs six days a week out of Crisfield.

The boat ride to Tangier can be quite stunning on a pretty day. The boats arrive at the active town dock, where fishing village life is still much the same as it has been for centuries.

The island was settled by Englishman John Crockett and his family in 1686. Tangier has a population of about 750 and most of them still speak with an Elizabethan accent.

The best way to explore tiny Tangier Island is by foot. It's about two and a half miles long and less than a mile wide.

Some walking tour highlights include: Tangier Museum, a great collection of island memorabilia; Hayne's Grocery, the

A Tangier Island fisherman and a fine catch of crabs

community supermarket; Tangier School, a twelve-grade schoolhouse; Tangier Airport, popular with small planes; and two churches, the Swain Memorial United Methodist Church and the New Testament Congregation.

To take home a Tangier Island memory, stop by Island Gifts at 59 North Main Street. Non-shoppers can relax on the front porch while others can look for decoys, miniature crab pots, seashells, nautical items, and much more.

But whether you're there for the day, for the night, or an entire weekend, be sure to head to Hilda Crockett's Chesapeake House. This Tangier Island landmark restaurant and inn was established by Hilda Crockett in 1939 and is now run by her two daughters, Betty Nohe and Edna Moore.

A meal at the Chesapeake House is a Tangier Island requirement. Patrons sit at long tables and are served family-style meals, with crab cakes, clam fritters, homemade bread, and pound cake among the many highlights.

The Chesapeake House also offers overnight lodging in comfortable rooms. The low rates include the big seafood dinner and breakfast. It completes the perfect Tangier Island visit.

Specifically: For further information about Tangier Island, contact the Eastern Shore of Virginia Chamber of Commerce at P.O. Box R, Melfa, VA 23410, 804-787-2460. For boats to Tangier Island, contact Tangier Island Cruises at 410-968-2338 or the Tangier Mail and Freight Service at 804-891-2240. Shoppers should head to Island Gifts, 804-891-2530. For memorable meals and lodging, contact Hilda Crockett's Chesapeake House at 804-891-2331.

Summer

14 A Wild Time on the Eastern Shore
Chincoteague

The mighty Chesapeake Bay separates Virginia's remote Eastern Shore from the rest of the state, making for a simpler way of life in places like Chincoteague and for people like Donald Leonard. But every July, Leonard and about 50,000 people (and more than 100 ponies) get wild in the island town of Chincoteague. The annual Chincoteague Volunteer Firemen's Carnival and Pony Round-up and Swim provides one of America's great island getaways.

Leonard, a local pony personality and saltwater cowboy, explains that the wild ponies of nearby Assateague Island have developed into a huge tourist draw, and that he himself has played a big role in this success.

"The pony penning each July involves rounding up the wild ponies on Assateague and then herding them across the sound to Chincoteague for an auction," he says, "but that's just the beginning of this wild time for me and many other locals and tourists.

"The pony penning started more than 200 years ago, but the modern era began in 1925," he says. "I'm the same age as the modern pony penning and carnival, so I guess you could say I'm a veteran at it. I've been very active with the fire company and I only recall missing one pony penning, back during World War II."

When Leonard's ancestors came to Chincoteague more than 300 years ago, he says, the horses were already there. Though some tales attribute the wild ponies on Assateague Island to a sunken Spanish galleon, most locals believe the current horses are descendants of those set loose on the island by settlers in the 1600s.

These horses were occasionally herded for claiming, branding, and harnessing. The round-up eventually developed into a time of much working, selling, eating, and drinking.

By the late 1800s, people were journeying to Chincoteague to see the round-up and to join in the celebrations. Big crowds in the early 1900s, along with two devastating fires in downtown Chincoteague, convinced the island residents that they needed better firefighting equipment and organization.

In 1925, the island's volunteer firemen took over the pony penning and carnival as a fund-raiser. That was also the start of the modern method of herding the ponies on Assateague and then driving them across the narrow channel for a short "swim" to Chincoteague.

The first "official" volunteer firemen's round-up, swim, and auction in 1925 was a huge success, with more than 15,000 people in attendance to see the penning and subsequent sale of about twenty colts, priced at $75.00 for males and $90.00 for females. The proceeds allowed the firemen to buy a new pump truck.

The Chincoteague Volunteer Fire Company eventually bought its own herd of horses, which it keeps on the Virginia portion of Assateague Island (now the Chincoteague National Wildlife Refuge). These saltwater cowboys maintain the

A wild pony on the beach at Chincoteague

health and welfare of the herd, under the guidance of refuge officials, a veterinarian, and animal welfare officials.

Though the pony penning and auction have become hugely popular, the carnival is the big money-raiser for the fire company. This traditional small-town carnival features several weekends and weekdays of carnival attractions, fireworks, entertainment, demonstrations, and tasty food.

Thanks to the pony penning, carnival, natural areas, wild ponies, and other attractions, Chincoteague has become a very popular island destination all year. The island features a wide array of accommodation options, from camping to quaint bed and breakfasts to full-service hotels. Seafood lovers will find plenty of places to enjoy the fresh bounties of the sea.

Specifically: Chincoteague is easily reached by taking US 13 south through the Maryland portion of the Eastern Shore or north through the Virginia portion. For further information, contact the Chincoteague Chamber of Commerce visitors center at P.O. Box 258, Chincoteague, VA 23336, 804-336-6161.

15 Colonial Williamsburg and the Rest of the Historic Triangle

Even in a state blessed with so much history to explore, Colonial Williamsburg and the nearby cities of Yorktown and Jamestown – the trio known as the Historic Triangle – are very special treats for the eye and the mind. Together they can provide many weekends of historical exploration. The summer provides the perfect opportunity for the entire family to experience an educational and enjoyable weekend, but you should visit this four-season destination every chance you have. More than 1 million visitors annually can't be wrong.

Colonial Williamsburg portrays the city as it appeared in the eighteenth century, on the eve of the Revolution. It covers 173 acres of the 220-acre town laid out in 1699 by Royal Governor Francis Nicholson.

Bisected by mile-long Duke of Gloucester Street, the historical area is enhanced by a 3,000-acre greenbelt. There are eighty-eight original structures, fifty major reconstructions, and forty exhibition buildings containing 225 rooms, with furnishings from a 100,000-item collection. There are also ninety acres of gardens and greens, fifteen exhibition sites, ten shops, twenty-one trade presentations, several museums, historic interpreters, and many special and ongoing programs. Another highlight is nearby Carter's Grove, which features a 1754 mansion, Wolstenholme Towne, a museum, slave quarters, and a reception center.

Any weekend should start with a stop at the informative visitors center. Opened in 1957, the visitors center provides parking, information, tickets, bus service, and reservations. Orientation begins with "Williamsburg – The Story of a Patriot," a thirty-five-minute film starring Jack Lord.

Visitors should plan to spend at least one night, and there are many excellent options, including: Williamsburg Inn,

51

*The handsome Governor's Palace
at Colonial Williamsburg*

Williamsburg Lodge and Conference Center, the Woodlands, the Governor's Inn, and unique tavern accommodations. Along with other dining options, operating taverns include Chowning's, Christiana Campbell's, Shields, and King's Arms. For shoppers, Merchants Square is an ideal place for that perfect gift or weekend memory.

There is a wide variety of ticket options for adults and children, as well as many package possibilities that include accommodations and dining.

Colonial Williamsburg also provides a perfect base for exploring Yorktown and Jamestown, the other two points of the Historic Triangle. Be prepared, however, to spend more than just a weekend exploring the historic riches of the area.

Yorktown, part of the Colonial National Historical Park, was the site of the last major battle of the Revolutionary War and the surrender of Lord Cornwallis to Gen. George Washington in 1781. A visitors center includes a film, museum, gift shop, rooftop overlook, and the start of a battlefield tour. The Yorktown Victory Center tells the story of the American Revolution through a documentary film, thematic exhibits, and outdoor living history.

Jamestown, also part of the Colonial National Historical Park, was the original site of the first permanent English settlement in the New World. This National Historic Site includes a visitors center with a film, museum, gift shop, reconstructed Glasshouse built in 1608, and ruins of the 1640s church tower, as well as the original town. At Jamestown Settlement, the settlers' story is told through a docudrama film, expansive indoor gallery exhibits, full-sized re-creations of ships, and outdoor settings where costumed interpreters portray life in Virginia at the beginning of the seventeenth century.

Specifically: To receive the excellent "Vacation Planner," contact Colonial Williamsburg at P.O. Box 1776, Williamsburg, VA 23187-1776, 804-229-1000 or 800-HISTORY. Contact the Colonial National Historical Park at P.O. Box 210, Yorktown, VA 23690, 804-898-3400. Contact the Jamestown-Yorktown Foundation at P.O. Drawer JF, Williamsburg, VA 23187, 804-253-4175.

16 The Tides Inn
Irvington

The Tides Inn is one of Virginia's (and America's) special destinations and the perfect place to head for a very special weekend. This Northern Neck mecca provides an elegant waterfront weekend retreat unlike any other in Virginia.

Captain John Smith may have said it best: "Within is a country that may have the prerogative over the most pleasant places known, for large and pleasant navigable rivers, heaven and earth never agreed better to frame a place for man's habitation."

Within this country that Smith loved is The Tides Inn. Ann Lee ("Miss Ann") and E. A. Stephens opened this hospitable resort on July 15, 1947, with forty-six rooms, a dining room, a bottle club (bar), and a dream. Now people from around the world dream of their next stay at The Tides Inn.

Located in the quiet community of Irvington on the shores of Carter's Creek, The Tides Inn offers an unsurpassed weekend combining relaxation and activity. You'll find tastefully appointed accommodations; unforgettable yacht cruises aboard the legendary *Miss Ann* and other boating possibilities; forty-five holes of highly rated golf; tennis on fast-dry competition or all-weather courts; dancing and honeymoon parties at the inviting Chesapeake Club; acclaimed meals graciously served in impeccable dining rooms; luncheons and cocktails at the poolside Summer House, aboard the yachts, or at Cap'n B's at the Golden Eagle golf club; elegant shopping; playrooms, bikes, and a beachside saltwater pool; unique evening entertainment; and an informal elegance and level of service that draw repeat visitors like few small resorts in the world.

The relaxing atmosphere of luxury—where coat and tie are still required after 6:30 P.M.—sets the scene for a unique stay. You can do as little (or as much) as you want during your weekend. During the day, your choices might include an oyster roast, a luncheon cruise, a welcome party hosted by the Stephens family, parlor games, and a movie.

In the evening, The Tides Inn dining experience provides the highlight for many guests. The headwaiter assigns you to a table for the duration of your visit. The friendly wait staff enhances the excellent meals prepared by the award-winning kitchen.

Any Tides Inn experience starts (and ends) with impeccable service from everyone at the resort, from the yacht captain to the gardener to the owner. The staff is the primary reason that entire families and generations of loyal guests have returned for more than twenty consecutive seasons. It's a great place to start a weekend tradition of your own.

Specifically: Contact The Tides Inn at Irvington, VA 22480; 804-438-5000 or 800-TIDES INN.

Tides Inn guests can also enjoy the dining and other facilities available at The Tides Lodge, located just across the water. This resort also provides a more casual Northern Neck weekend option, which is ideal for many golfers and boaters. Contact The Tides Lodge at Box 4, Irvington, VA 22480, 804-438-6000 or 800-248-4337.

17 Founders Inn
Virginia Beach

The Founders Inn and Conference Center provides a perfect Virginia Beach escape from the twentieth-century stress and strain of daily living. Guests will find it an ideal way to spend a stress-free weekend. This 249-room resort blends the quiescence and quaintness of early colonial days with the amenities of a modern resort.

Located adjacent to the headquarters of its parent company, the Christian Broadcasting Network (CBN), the resort has attracted hundreds of thousands of guests in search of a peaceful getaway. Though many of the guests come along with a religious group, individuals are warmly welcomed and are coming in record numbers.

One of the reasons this $35.5-million historical replica is so unique is its totally wholesome and health-conscious atmosphere. Alcohol and smoking are only occasionally allowed.

In keeping with the healthful philosophy, the founders of the Founders Inn constructed a two-story multimillion-dollar health club that offers cutting-edge wellness programs delivered by a staff of trained and certified physical fitness professionals. The club has an aerobic center and weight room, two racquetball courts, tennis courts, a quarter-mile walking track, saunas, locker rooms, and numerous individual and group exercise programs, as well as personalized fitness evaluations.

Guests can exercise their palates in one of two superb dining areas, including the Swan Terrace, an elegant full-service restaurant featuring American regional cuisine and popular buffets.

The CBN studios are just a five-minute walk from the hotel. On the same grounds as the Founders Inn, the red-brick three-story CBN building is capped by a white three-tiered steeple. Inside the columned entrance are broadcast studios that reach out to nearly every country in the world.

Each day, religious and secular audiences alike show up for the live broadcast of "The 700 Club," hosted by Pat Robertson, founder and chairman of CBN. The spectacle is an exercise in synchronization. Lights dim, then brighten as a rapt audience looks on from the darkened gallery.

The studio is cooled to sweater-weather temperatures, but the audience is warm to the scene unfolding before them. More than once, heads are bowed in prayer during the remarkable proceedings.

A visit to the CBN studios, including excellent tours, is another bonus for Founders Inn guests. It's just part of a special weekend, leaving those who stay at the Founders Inn at peace with the world, if only for a few days.

Specifically: Contact the Founders Inn at 5641 Indian River Road, Virginia Beach, VA 23464, 804-424-5511 or 800-926-4466.

18 Fore!

You don't have to flee to Florida to find great golf. The Old Dominion offers enough golf to keep any hacker happy for many weekend rounds without ever leaving the state.

In conjunction with the Virginia Tourism Development Group, the Golf Virginia Resorts Association provides an excellent guide to more than 130 of Virginia's public, semi-private, and resort courses. Along with introductory material and a regional map, the brochure lists course names, addresses, phone numbers, and course details.

On any pleasant weekend, there's a wide range of public possibilities in the Richmond capital region. Whether you want to play the popular Joe Lee design at The Crossings, putt on the area's largest greens at Confederate Hills, or go for the convenience of Oak Hill just out Patterson Avenue, there's a scorecard waiting.

Other public courses in the Richmond area include: Belmont Golf Course in Henrico County; the Dan Maples layout at the Birkdale Golf Course; Brookwoods Golf Club in Quinton; Glenwood Golf Club northeast on Creighton Road; River's Bend Golf and Country Club running parallel to the James River in Chester; Spring Lake Golf Club north on US 301; and Sycamore Creek Golf Course out in Manakin. If you want some quick work on your game, head for one of many driving ranges or try Windy Hill par 3 and other facilities.

A little further afield, additional public options include: The Lakes in Highland Springs; Mill Quarter Plantation near Powhatan; and the Prince George Golf Course in Disputanta. With so many courses, it's just a matter of calling for a weekend tee time.

Of course, there are many private and semiprivate possibilities in the Richmond metropolitan area. The golf tradition has led to many fine country clubs for members and
their guests to enjoy, including: the Brandermill Country
Club; the Country Club of Virginia; the Dominion Country
Club at Wyndham; Hanover Country Club; Hermitage Country Club; Jefferson Lakeside Country Club; Oak Hill Country
Club; Richmond Country Club; and Salisbury Country Club.

In Williamsburg, Kingsmill Resort (see Chapter 7) continues to offer great golf vacations. In addition to Kingsmill's
three eighteen-hole championship courses, another attraction is the Bray Links, a nine-hole par 3 course ideal for practicing short games.

Ford's Colony Country Club is quickly becoming known
as the perfect place to head for Dan Maples golf and one of
the top golf resort restaurants in the country. With nine additional holes recently opened and creative options in the
Dining Room, this Williamsburg resort is one of the state's
biggest success stories on and off the links.

The new nine brings the Ford's Colony total to forty-five,
all designed by Dan Maples. This 2,500-acre residential golf
resort community now features exclusive homes, large home-
sites, a full fitness center, and satisfying dining.

The Colonial Williamsburg complex (see Chapter 15)
offers some great golf to go with its history. The restored
eighteenth-century colonial capital of Virginia, a world-
renowned living history museum, sports two well-known
championship golf courses, an executive-length course, four
hotels (including the five-star Williamsburg Inn), thirteen
restaurants, and many other resort amenities.

Visiting golfers can take advantage of golf package plans
that include unlimited golf on both Golden Horseshoe
courses and the Spotswood course, lodging in Colonial

Williamsburg hotels, and daily use of a cart and practice balls. For further package information, call 800-HISTORY.

A bit further down the interstate, the Virginia Beach area is perfect for a great golf getaway, with its convenient mid-Atlantic location, mild weather conditions, legendary beach resort amenities, and a large variety of golf courses.

Virginia Beach proves that a golf vacation today doesn't need to be full of tee-time hassles, crowded accommodations, and high prices. Golf in Virginia Beach means uncrowded greens, a large selection of resort hotels, and value-packed packages.

Some of the most popular courses in the Virginia Beach area include Hell's Point, Honey Bee, Owl's Creek, and Red Wing Lake. Along with many other places to play, many hotels offer great packages to golfers, including accommodations, greens fees, and other amenities.

A free copy of the "Virginia Beach Golf Guide," published by the city and the Department of Convention and Visitor Development, is available by calling 800-VA BEACH.

The Tides Inn (see Chapter 7) on the Chesapeake Bay is another popular golf destination for Richmonders. This complete resort getaway includes golf, tennis, a fitness center, family activities, and cruises on the resort's yacht. More possibilities are available nearby at Tides Lodge.

In the center of the state, Wintergreen Resort (see Chapter 2) offers mountain golf at its finest and the state's only full-service golf school, the Wintergreen Golf Academy. The golf is great on either Devil's Knob, an Ellis Maples course, or Rees Jones's award-winning Stoney Creek. But this year-round resort in the Blue Ridge Mountains has much more to offer, including fishing, tennis, the Wintergarden Spa, horseback riding, and very popular mountain biking.

The Wintergreen Golf Academy is run by international

professional and teacher Graeme Oliver. The two-, three-, and four-day packages cater to all levels of players and offer individualized instruction in small groups (4:1 student to instructor ratio).

Even further west, The Homestead (see Chapter 45) continues to provide a legendary golf experience. Since its purchase by Dallas-based Club Resorts, a company boasting dozens of golf resorts and a great track record, The Homestead is sure to become an even better golf destination.

Many additions and updates have been completed at The Homestead, including renovations of The Homestead Course, a new practice facility, and the opening of the Golf Advantage School, already a successful institution at Pinehurst.

Many other state hotels and resorts also feature golf packages. Dedicated duffers should explore the options at places throughout the state, such as Shenandoah Crossing in Gordonsville, Staunton's Ingleside Red Carpet Inn, Luray Caverns, Bryce Resort, Massanutten, the Westpark Hotel, and Leesburg's Landsdowne Conference Resort (see Chapter 36).

There are also many public options around the state. Some popular choices with Richmond golfers on the road include Afton's Swannanoa, Hadensville's Royal Virginia, Norfolk's Ocean View, and The Links at Natural Bridge. Almost all metropolitan areas in the state offer one or more public courses.

Specifically: The brochure covering Virginia golf is a great way to begin research for a Virginia golf weekend. Interested golfers who call 800-93 BACK 9 (800-932-2259) will receive the "Virginia Golf" guide, a "Virginia is for Lovers Travel Guide," and a state highway map. Further information can be obtained by contacting the Virginia Division of

Tourism at 901 East Byrd Street, Richmond, VA 23219, 804-786-4484 or 800-932-5827.

In the following list, CC stands for Country Club and GC stands for Golf Course.

Afton	Swannanoa CC	703-942-9877
Alexandria	Greendale GC	703-971-6170
Alexandria	Pinecrest No. 1 GC	703-941-1061
Basye	Bryce Resort GC	703-856-2121
Blacksburg	Blacksburg Municipal GC	703-961-1137
Bluefield	Richwood GC	703-322-4575
Bracey	River Ridge Golf & Campground	804-636-2989
Brookneal	Hat Creek GC	804-376-2292
Callao	Village Green GC	804-529-6332
Cape Charles	Northampton CC	804-331-8423
Centreville	Twin Lakes CC	703-631-9099
Charlottesville	McIntyre Park GC	804-977-4111
Charlottesville	Meadowcreek GC	804-977-0615
Chatham	Cedar's CC	804-656-9909
Chesapeake	Seven Springs GC	804-436-2512
Clarksville	Kinderton CC	804-374-8822
Clifford	Winton CC	804-946-7336
Clifton	Twin Lakes GC	703-631-9099
Clifton Forge	Cliftondale CC	703-862-2081
Coeburn	Dan Hall Mtn. Resort	703-395-2487
Covington	Alleghany CC	703-862-5789
Damascus	Deer Field GC	703-475-5649
Danville	Ringold GC	804-799-8728
Ewing	Monte Vista GC	703-861-4014
Fairfax	Burke Lake GC	703-323-6600
Fairfax	Penderbrook GC	703-385-3700

Fairfax	Jefferson GC	703-941-1062
Fancy Gap	Skyland Lakes GC	703-728-4923
Farmville	Longwood GC	804-395-2613
Farmville	Wedgewood CC	804-392-6656
Fredericksburg	Lee's Hill	703-891-1091
Fredericksburg	Shannon Green GC	703-786-8385
Front Royal	Bowling Green CC	703-635-2024
Front Royal	Front Royal CC	703-636-9061
Front Royal	Shenandoah Valley GC	703-636-2641
Galax	Blue Ridge CC	703-236-9845
Gasburg	Thisuldu GC	703-577-2442
Gate City	Scott County GC	703-452-4168
Gloucester	Gloucester CC	804-693-2662
Greenbackville	Captain's Cove GC	804-824-3465
Hadensville	Royal Virginia GC	804-784-4589
Hampton	Eaglewood GC	804-764-4547
Hampton	Hampton Golf & Tennis Ctr	804-727-1195
Hampton	Hamptons GC	804-766-9148
Harrisonburg	Lakeview GC	703-434-8937
Harrisonburg	Massanutten Village GC	703-289-9441
Herndon	Herndon Centennial GC	703-471-5769
Hopewell	Jordan Point CC	804-458-0141
Hot Springs	The Homestead	703-839-7739
Irvington	Tides Inn – Golden Eagle	804-438-5501
Irvington	Tides Lodge – Tides Tartan	804-438-6000
Jonesville	Cedar Hill GC	703-346-1535
Laurel Fork	Olde Mill GC	703-398-2638
Leesburg	Algonkian Park	703-450-4655
Leesburg	Goose Creek	703-729-2500
Leesburg	Westpark Hotel & GC	703-777-7023
Leesburg	Landsdowne Conf. Resort	703-729-8400
Lorton	Pohick Bay Regional Park	703-339-8585
Luray	Caverns CC	703-743-7111

Lynchburg	Cedar Hills GC	804-239-1512
Lynchburg	Colonial Hills GC	804-525-3954
Lynchburg	Ivy Hill GC	804-525-2680
Lynchburg	London Downs GC	804-525-4653
Lynchburg	Poplar Forest GC	804-525-0473
Manassas	Prince William GC	703-754-7111
Manassas	Manassas Hills GC	703-368-2028
Marion	Holston Hills CC	703-783-7484
Martinsville	Beaver Hill GC	703-632-1526
Montpelier	The Hollows	804-798-2949
Mt. Holly	Bushfield GC	804-472-2602
Natural Bridge	The Links GC	703-291-4653
New Market	Shenvalee GC	703-740-3181
Newport News	Deer Run GC	804-886-2848
Newport News	Kiln Creek GC	804-874-0526
Nokesville	Prince William GC	703-754-7111
Norfolk	Eagle Haven GC	804-464-8526
Norfolk	Lake Wright GC	804-461-2246
Norfolk	Ocean View GC	804-480-2094
Norfolk	Sewell's Point GC	804-444-5572
Pembroke	Castle Rock GC	703-626-7275
Petersburg	Lee Park GC	804-733-5667
Petersburg	Prince George GC	804-991-2251
Portsmouth	City Park GC	804-393-8005
Portsmouth	Bide-A-Wee	804-399-9562
Portsmouth	Sleepy Hole GC	804-393-5050
Rappahannock	Four Winds GC	804-742-5647
Reston	Reston GC	703-620-9333
Richmond	Belmont GC	804-266-4929
Richmond	Bermuda GC	804-458-9974
Richmond	Birkdale GC	804-739-8800
Richmond	Brandermill CC	804-744-1185
Richmond	Brookwoods GC	804-737-0519

Richmond	Confederate Hills	804-737-4716
Richmond	Country Club of Virginia	804-288-2891
Richmond	The Crossings	804-226-2254
Richmond	Dominion CC at Wyndham	804-360-1200
Richmond	Glenwood GC	804-226-1793
Richmond	Hanover CC	804-798-8381
Richmond	Hermitage CC	804-784-5234
Richmond	Jefferson Lakeside CC	804-266-2780
Richmond	The Lakes	804-737-4716
Richmond	Mill Quarter Plantation	804-598-4221
Richmond	Oak Hill CC	804-784-5592
Richmond	Pine Lakes	804-226-9859
Richmond	Richmond CC	804-784-5272
Richmond	River's Bend Golf & CC	804-530-1000
Richmond	Salisbury CC	804-794-6841
Richmond	Spring Lake GC	804-226-9859
Richmond	Sycamore Creek GC	804-784-3544
Richmond	Windy Hill	804-794-7193
Roanoke	Blue Hills GC	703-344-7848
Roanoke	Botetourt CC	703-992-1451
Roanoke	Countryside GC	703-563-0391
Roanoke	Ole Monterey GC	703-563-0400
Salem	City of Salem GC	703-387-9802
Salem	Hanging Rock GC	703-389-8193
Saltville	Saltville GC	703-496-4716
Smith Mountain Lake	Chestnut Creek GC	703-721-4214
Smith Mountain Lake	Mariner's GC	703-297-7888
Smithfield	Smithfield Downs GC	804-357-3101
South Boston	Green's Folly GC	804-572-4998
Staunton	Country Club of Staunton	703-248-7273
Staunton	Gypsy Hill GC	703-387-9802

Staunton	Ingleside Red Carpet Inn	703-248-1201
Stuart	Gorden Trent GC	703-694-3805
Suffolk	Suffolk GC	804-539-6298
Surry	Surry GC	804-357-3101
Tappahannock	Woodside CC	804-443-4060
Virginia Beach	Bow Creek GC	804-431-3763
Virginia Beach	Cypress Point GC	804-490-8822
Virginia Beach	Hell's Point	804-721-3400
Virginia Beach	Honey Bee GC	804-471-2768
Virginia Beach	Kempsville Greens	804-474-8441
Virginia Beach	Owl's Creek	804-428-2800
Virginia Beach	Red Wing Lake GC	804-437-4845
Virginia Beach	Stumpy Lake GC	804-467-6119
Warrenton	South Wales GC	804-347-1401
Waynesboro	Shields Par Three	703-943-7283
White Stone	Windjammer GC	804-435-1166
Williamsburg	Ford's Colony	804-258-4130
Williamsburg	Golden Horseshoe	804-229-1000
Williamsburg	Kingsmill GC	804-253-3906
Williamsburg	Spotswood GC	804-229-1000
Winchester	Carpers Valley	703-662-4319
Winchester	The Summit	703-888-4188
Wintergreen	Devils Knob GC	804-325-2200
Wintergreen	Stoney Creek GC	804-325-2200
Woodbridge	Lakeridge GC	703-494-5564

19 Smith Mountain Lake
Moneta

If hot summer days turn your thoughts to cool mountain lakes, you'll want to try a dip – or a whole weekend – at Smith Mountain Lake.

Nestled in the mountains of southwest Virginia, Smith Mountain Lake is known as "The Jewel of the Blue Ridge." It's forty miles long, offers more than 500 miles of shoreline, and covers about 20,000 fun-filled acres.

Since the Smith Mountain Dam's completion in 1966, the lake has become a thriving year-round residential and resort community. It makes for a great weekend on and off the water.

Water sports attract thousands of weekend visitors to Smith Mountain Lake annually. More than twenty-five different marinas dot the lakeshore and sailboats, motor boats, jet-skis, pontoons, bass boats, and windsurfers are all welcome.

Fishing, waterskiing, parasailing, swimming in the clean water, or just relaxing on one of many beaches are also popular activities. Smith Mountain Lake State Park features a public beach for swimming, as well as picnic sites and hiking trails.

On dry land, Smith Mountain Lake provides a beautiful backdrop for the four golf courses in the area. Horseback riding along scenic trails is also quite popular.

Weekend visitors have a wide range of accommodation options, including luxurious townhouses and condominiums, private homes, a lodge, bed and breakfasts, motels, cabins, and campgrounds. There is some type of lodging available for all tastes and budgets. For a special weekend stay, head for the Manor at Taylor's Store, a unique bed and breakfast with a melange of rustic and modern touches.

Weekend dining choices are also varied, but two of the most popular are a romantic dinner overlooking the water or a dinnertime cruise. Casual dining and fast-food restaurants are also available near the lake, as is grocery shopping for those weekenders with kitchen facilities in their accommodations. Some of the best views and meals are available at The Landing.

Specifically: Contact the Smith Mountain Lake Chamber of Commerce at 2 Bridgewater Plaza, Moneta, VA 24121, 703-721-1203 or 800-676-8203.

Contact the Manor at Taylor's Store at 703-721-3951. Contact The Landing at 703-721-3028.

20 Virginia Is for (Beach) Lovers

Just as each grain of sand is distinctively different, each of Virginia's beaches is unique. From the resort life at Virginia Beach to the quiet calm of Chincoteague, Virginia is for lovers . . . of beaches. There's simply nothing better than a summer weekend at the beach.

Virginia's beaches serve up the best of summer. Images of the seaside, sand, beach blankets, sand castles, beach balls, suntan oil, water sports, and much more become reality for Virginia beach bums.

At twenty-eight miles, Virginia Beach is the Atlantic coast's longest run of resort beach, and it's easy to reach. The interstate network puts Virginia Beach within a day's drive for the eastern third of the country, and major airlines offer daily flights into nearby Norfolk International Airport.

The most popular stretch of sand in the Old Dominion, Virginia Beach always has something new to offer the visitor. These days, the newest attraction is literally the new beach – the result of "Operation Big Beach," which created almost three miles of newer, bigger, and better beach from Tenth to Forty-eighth Street. The addition makes the fine-grained sand even more inviting. Those who aren't on the bigger beach are often on the new and lively boardwalk running parallel to it.

The sand and surf are Virginia Beach's major attractions, but there's lots more to do in this resort area, such as the Virginia Beach Maritime Historical Museum. Located right on the boardwalk at Twenty-fourth Street, the building was originally a U.S. Lifesaving/Coast Guard Station.

Today, the museum houses interesting nautical artifacts, scrimshaw, ship models, photographs, marine memorabilia, and a great gift shop for those who want to take a little bit of the Atlantic home with them. Make sure to check out the

Summer means head for the beach

Norwegian Lady Statue nearby, which commemorates the tragic wreck of the *Dictator* off the shores of Virginia Beach in 1891.

Saltwater lovers should also consider an oceanfront cruise or deep-sea fishing. The boats leave from marinas at Rudee or Lynnhaven Inlet. Afterwards, enjoy the fresh catch at one of the many popular seafood restaurants in the area.

Accommodations abound in the Virginia Beach vicinity, from luxurious beachfront resorts to inexpensive inns off the main drag. It's best to make reservations during special events, like the Boardwalk Art Show, the Neptune Festival, or Norfolk's Harborfest.

But the Virginia Beach area doesn't have a monopoly on Virginia beach fun. There are lots of other options along Virginia's miles of coastline. Nearby, check out quieter Sandbridge, Grandview, Buckroe, or Ocean View. Outdoors lovers should head to undeveloped False Cape State Park (five miles south of Sandbridge) or Seashore State Park and Natural Area, Virginia's most visited state park, at Cape Henry in Virginia Beach.

For an even more unique Virginia Beach experience, head across one of the world's great engineering feats, the seventeen-mile Chesapeake Bay Bridge-Tunnel, where another world of beaches and life await along the Eastern Shore. The islands of Chincoteague and Assateague (see Chapter 14) offer the beach lover many miles of solitary sand. There are more than forty miles of unspoiled beach, lots of wildlife, and a real sense of what beach life was like in Virginia's distant past.

Though much more sedate than many resort beaches, there's lots to do on and near the islands. Nature lovers should explore Chincoteague National Refuge or Assateague

National Seashore. Others will discover the decorative wildfowl carvings in the quaint shops, as well as the oyster and wildfowl museums.

Just about the only time these two islands see large crowds is during a festival, and then it's the more the merrier. Of course, everyone should see the annual Fireman's Pony Swim and Carnival in July (see Chapter 14). But seafood lovers should also check out Chincoteague's seafood festival in May or the Oyster Festival in October.

Over on the Chesapeake Bay side, Cape Charles offers old-time beach town life with working watermen and old Victorian homes offering quaint lodging. The small beach at Cape Charles is ideal for quiet strolls.

However, the Atlantic Ocean and Chesapeake Bay aren't the only bodies of water offering the beach life to Virginia visitors. Nine state parks feature swimming beaches in the southwest and central parts of the state. In the southwest, inland beach bums head for Claytor Lake, Douthat, Hungry Mother, and New River. In the central region, there's Bear Creek Lake, Fairy Stone, Holliday Lake, Twin Lakes, and Smith Mountain Lake.

Specifically: For further information about Virginia's beaches, contact Virginia Beach at 800-VA BEACH; the Eastern Shore Tourism Commission at 804-787-2460; or the Virginia State Parks system at 804-786-1712.

21 Edgar Cayce's Association for Research and Enlightenment, Virginia Beach

The legend of Edgar Cayce lives in Virginia Beach, making for a unique way to spend a weekend. Many people know about Edgar Cayce, the most documented psychic of the twentieth century, but most don't know of the legacy he left in Virginia Beach.

Until his death in 1945, Edgar Cayce was one of the most remarkable psychic talents of all time. As a young man, Cayce found he was able to enter into a self-induced sleep state, enabling him to answer questions or give discourses about almost any subject matter or topic. These discourses, which became known as "readings," numbered more than 14,000 and have been intensively researched for more than a century.

Most of the questions Cayce answered concerned physical ailments. Given the name and location of an individual anywhere in the world, he could correctly describe the person's condition and outline treatment procedures. Cayce discussed the interconnectedness of attitudes, emotions, and the physical body, and eventually became known as the "father of holistic medicine."

Cayce moved to Virginia Beach in 1925 and founded the Association for Research and Enlightenment (A.R.E.) in 1931. Though begun as the international headquarters for his work, the A.R.E. has become much more for members, visitors, and anyone interested in psychic phenomena.

Visitors are always welcome to the A.R.E. headquarters, but the community has grown into a network of individuals who offer conferences, educational activities, and fellowship around the world. People of every age are invited to participate in programs that focus on topics such as holistic health, dreams, reincarnation, ESP, the power of the mind, meditation, and personal spirituality.

In addition to study groups and various activities, the A.R.E. offers membership benefits and services, a bimonthly magazine, a newsletter, extracts from the Cayce readings, international tours, a massage-school curriculum, an impressive volunteer network, a retreat-type camp for children and adults, an affiliation with Atlantic University (which offers a master's degree program in Transpersonal Studies), and A.R.E. contacts around the world.

Though you don't have to visit Virginia Beach to enjoy the benefits of the A.R.E., it's well worth the trip. The A.R.E. visitors center has become an Edgar Cayce mecca for good reason. A weekend at the A.R.E. can (and probably will) change your life.

"I think the A.R.E. is one of the best-kept travel secrets in America," says Robert J. Grant, the A.R.E.'s coordinator for public information. "While a number of television and radio programs, books, and articles have been published about the work of Edgar Cayce, a lot of people don't realize how ideal Virginia Beach and the A.R.E. are for a weekend with something different."

The visitors center is located just one block from the Atlantic Ocean, close to Virginia Beach's tourist accommodations and beach facilities. More than 40,000 people attend tours, conferences, or workshops at the A.R.E. visitors center every year.

Though Edgar Cayce died fifty years ago, his legend lives in Virginia Beach. It's always fun to go to the beach, but in Virginia Beach, the A.R.E. beckons anyone interested in Cayce and the work that continues today.

Specifically: For more information about the A.R.E., contact P.O. Box 595, Sixty-seventh and Atlantic Avenues, Virginia Beach, VA 23451-0595, 804-428-3588. For more information about the Virginia Beach area, contact the Virginia Beach Information Center at 800-VA BEACH (822-3224).

22 Making Weekend Waves in Norfolk

For more than 300 years, the sea has sustained and romanced Norfolk. Visitors here will find a progressive city on the move, featuring exciting new attractions, ever-gracious hospitality and charm, and an eye-popping display of U.S. Navy warships, foreign merchant ships, fishing vessels, and weekend pleasure craft.

Norfolk is also visitor-friendly. While it offers a one-mile, self-guided tour of city attractions, for example, the tenderfoot and walk-weary can take a trolley, which runs from May through September every hour on the hour and stops at each attraction.

Many visitors discover that the $23.5 million Waterside is a delightful place to begin and end any visit to Norfolk. The recently expanded festival marketplace there now has almost 150 shops along the waterfront. Culinary delights abound here, ranging from homemade fudge prepared by musical chefs to fresh, succulent seafood.

Outside, a brick promenade leads to the Waterside Marina. During warm months, people gather for music, dancing, and a moonlight stroll on the pier. From the promenade, visitors can arrange for harbor tours on a variety of vessels: the *Carrie B,* a Mississippi-styled paddle wheeler; the *American Rover,* a three-masted schooner; the *Norfolk Rebel,* the first-of-its-kind sailing tugboat; and the *Spirit of Norfolk,* the largest cruise ship in Virginia, offering lunch, dinner, and moonlight cruises.

Town Point Park, a six-and-a-half-acre waterfront park next to the Waterside, hosts 200 free events each year. These fun-filled affairs include weekly TGIF parties, Norfolk's annual Harborfest celebration, the Virginia Wine Festival,

Oktoberfest, the Bluebeard Pirate Jamboree, and the Summer Family Movie Series.

The new Waterside Convention Center and adjacent Waterside Marriott Hotel are two of the newest gems to shine in the Norfolk crown of attractions. The $52 million complex offers weekend visitors upscale accommodations and amenities. Located just one block from Norfolk's working harbor, the convention center and 405-room Marriott connect to The Waterside Festival Marketplace.

Beyond Town Point Park, travelers can head to $40 million Nauticus, a premier maritime attraction that just opened in 1993. The three-level, 120,000-square-foot facility features one-of-a-kind interactive exhibits that allow visitors to participate in a marine discovery adventure.

The Douglas MacArthur Memorial presents the perfect opportunity to reflect on World War II and the role this controversial war hero played. Norfolk's 1850 courthouse, General MacArthur's final resting place, also houses eleven galleries of memorabilia tracing the general's life and military career. Among the items on display are surrender documents signed by Japanese Emperor Hirohito, the general's trademark corncob pipe, and even his official limousine, a 1950 Chrysler Crown Imperial. A newly renovated theater shows a twenty-two-minute film featuring historic action clips.

Like General MacArthur, Walter P. Chrysler Jr. adopted Norfolk as his home, and in 1971, the automobile heir gave the Norfolk Museum of Arts and Sciences his magnificent and extensive art collection. Renamed the Chrysler Museum, it showcases the works of masters from Cezanne to Warhol, as well as many other world-famous works of art.

And if it's ships you long to see, the Norfolk Naval Base is home port to more than 125 of them, plus fifty aircraft squadrons and sixty-five shore-based military activities. The base opened in 1917 on 474 acres, has now grown to 5,200 sprawling acres, and has played a major role in the history of the military.

Norfolk Naval Base tour tickets and bus departures are available at Norfolk's Waterside from March to December and at the Naval Base Tour Office year-round. Base personnel conduct the excellent tours on and off the tour buses, providing an insider's view of the base.

Tour highlights include the massive ships along the waterfront, the huge drydocks, the historic houses on Dillingham and Willoughby Boulevards, and the major military facilities throughout the base.

The fleet located along the waterfront is awe-inspiring with its vast array of aircraft carriers, submarines, cruisers, destroyers, amphibious ships, and support and logistic ships. The base is home port to two classes of attack submarines (Sturgeon and Los Angeles), as well as conventional and nuclear-powered aircraft carriers.

Each year, thousands of military personnel and tons of cargo pass through Norfolk on their way to and from destinations all over the world. Several times each year, the station also hosts ships and sailors of foreign navies that visit Hampton Roads.

Among the highlights of the land-based sights to see in Norfolk are the historic houses on Dillingham and Willoughby Boulevards. The homes were built in 1907 for the Jamestown Exposition, which commemorated the 300th anniversary of the English settlement in Jamestown. Contingents from twenty-one states built the structures, and each building represented the state's individual architectural style of the early 1900s. In 1917, President Woodrow Wilson signed a bill allowing the U.S. Navy to purchase the property and maintain the stately homes.

Over in Portsmouth, more military history awaits. The Portsmouth Naval Shipyard Museum was established in 1949 in the shipyard and was later moved to its current waterfront site to make it more accessible.

This comprehensive museum covers local and naval history, from pre–Civil War times to modern events. It is simply packed with displays and artifacts from the history of this centuries-old southern port, and deserves hours of wandering among the exhibits.

There are many ship models and items relating to the armed forces of the area, as well as exhibits portraying the lifestyle of eighteenth- and nineteenth-century Portsmouth. It's a virtual sea of naval history.

Just around the corner, visitors are drawn to the bright red Lightship Museum in the lightship *Portsmouth* – not a typical location for a museum. Lightships like this, with lights fixed to their masts, were once used in addition to standard lighthouses, to help mariners avoid dangerous shoals or enter harbors safely at night. This museum ship has been restored to its original 1915 condition. Visitors can board the vessel to see how the men of the Lightship Service lived during their many months at sea.

Other popular weekend options in Norfolk include: the Hermitage Foundation Museum, a Tudor-style mansion that now features Chinese tomb figures and relics from Czar Alexander's private collection; the d'Art Center, welcoming visitors to view sculptors, painters, jewelry makers, and textile artists as they work; the Virginia Zoological Park; the Norfolk Botanical Garden, which hosts the International Azalea Festival each April; and performances by the Virginia Symphony and the Virginia State Company.

Specifically: For more information about the area, contact the Norfolk Convention and Visitors Bureau, 236 East Plume Street, Norfolk, VA 23510, 804-441-1852 or 800-368-3097 or the Portsmouth Convention and Visitors Bureau, 505 Crawford Street, Ste. 2, Portsmouth, VA 23704, 804-393-5327 or 800-PORTS-VA.

23 A Weekend for the Kids

Throughout Virginia, weekend attractions are catering to kids. It's the perfect way for a family to spend a new kind of weekend in the Old Dominion.

The Historic Triangle (see Chapter 15) offers a great family weekend destination. Parents can explore their Colonial ties while the kids can earn a free patch and certificate in the Colonial National Historical Park's Junior Ranger Programs. Parents and children alike will want to engage in Colonial Williamsburg's various activity stations.

Learning time gives way to fun time at Virginia's theme parks, geared to entertaining children and adults of all ages with rides, shows, and shops. Options include Williamsburg's Busch Gardens and Water Country USA, Ocean Breeze Fun Park in Virginia Beach, and Paramount's Kings Dominion, just forty minutes north of Richmond.

The Hampton Roads area (see Chapter 24), just south of Williamsburg, is the perfect place to find a blend of attractions for kids and kids at heart. Among the most popular attractions is the Virginia Air and Space Center, where kids can project their own images into a replica of an official NASA spacesuit or simulate a rocket launch sequence.

In nearby Newport News, families can talk to the native animals at the Virginia Living Museum or discover the "Age of Exploration" exhibit at the Mariners' Museum. And children especially enjoy the hands-on displays about the Chesapeake Bay.

Across the James River, kids will love the Children's Museum in Portsmouth, where the principles of physics and architecture are demonstrated with soap bubbles and building blocks. Parents can get involved in participatory family activities like Kids' Corner or visit the Arts Center next door.

In Norfolk (see Chapter 22), families can enjoy the Grand Tour, a two-day tour designed especially for them that includes the Portsmouth Children's Museum. Other tour attractions include Norfolk's naval base, Busch Gardens, and the Virginia Zoological Park, with its rare white rhinos.

Just across the Chesapeake Bay is Virginia's Eastern Shore and Chincoteague, where families can cheer the herd of wild ponies as they swim the Assateague Channel the fourth week in July during the Annual Pony Swim and Auction (see Chapter 14). Throughout the spring and summer, the Chincoteague National Wildlife Refuge and Assateague National Seashore also host tours, safaris, cruises, and walks, as well as endangered species programs and other special events ideal for families.

City weekends offer a wealth of activities to choose from, but a Richmond trip (see Chapter 1) should start with the Children's Museum. With its mission "to expand children's awareness and respect for the world," the museum engages children from ages two to twelve in ten diverse hands-on exhibits, including TV Studio WRCM, where budding anchors and sportscasters can "broadcast" the news.

Youngsters and oldsters alike should check out Maymont Park with its farmyard, and should catch the exhibits, experiments, games, and programs at Richmond's Science Museum and the Children's Center in the Virginia Museum of Fine Arts. Be sure to stop at the museum gift shops to find unusual gifts for children.

Sites to see on the northern Virginia side of the national capital include the Arlington National Cemetery, where parents can share their personal memories at the gravesite of John F. Kennedy and watch the Changing of the Guard ceremony at the Tomb of the Unknowns.

Finally, make weekend plans to attend the International

Children's Festival, held in late summer just west of Arlington in Vienna's Wolf Trap Farm Park. It's a great way to spend a Virginia weekend with the family.

Specifically: For more information about weekend activities for families, contact: Colonial Williamsburg, 804-220-7645 or 800-HISTORY; Busch Gardens, 804-253-3350; Water Country USA, 804-229-9300 or 800-343-SWIM; Ocean Breeze Fun Park, 804-422-4444; Paramount's Kings Dominion 804-876-5000; Virginia Air and Space Center, 804-727-0800; Virginia Living Museum, 804-595-1900; The Mariners' Museum

Children's Museum, 804-595-0368; Portsmouth Children's Museum, 804-393-8983; Chincoteague Chamber of Commerce visitors center, 804-336-6161; Richmond Children's Museum, 804-788-4949; Maymont Park, 804-358-7166; Science Museum of Virginia, 804-367-1013; Virginia Museum of Fine Arts, 804-367-0844; and the Arlington County visitors center, 703-358-5720 or 800-677-6267.

24 Military Secrets
Hampton/Newport News

It's only natural that the Hampton/Newport News area should have so much military heritage to explore. Years of armed forces presence in such a small space means that there's lots of military history to see.

Well-situated on a strategic peninsula, the Hampton/Newport News area has been home to many military bases and huge shipbuilding facilities and has been a port of embarkation and debarkation for troops throughout American history. Much of this history can be explored today, with many museums and sightseeing possibilities.

The War Memorial Museum of Virginia provides a unique look at the state's role in World War II and other conflicts. Inside this fascinating museum, the saga of military history unfolds through more than 50,000 artifacts that document American wars from 1775 to the present.

Since 1923, the museum's high-quality displays have drawn military history buffs from around the world. Popular items include an 1883 brass Gatling Gun, a portion of the Dachau Concentration Camp wall, a World War I Renault Char I tank, and a Civil War blockade-runner's uniform. There are also hundreds of other uniforms, insignias, vehicles, weapons, and accoutrements on display.

One very popular attraction is the "40/8" boxcar, a gift from France to the Commonwealth of Virginia after World War II. This narrow boxcar got its name because it could carry forty soldiers or eight horses. But today, it carries an exhibit detailing the story of the impact of the war on the area, including photographs of embarking and debarking troops, various peninsula military facilities, an original copy of the World War I jazz tune "Newport News Blues", and personal items from Virginia's Twenty-ninth Division.

Also on display are many unusual items related to America's wartime efforts. One area, for instance, is solely devoted to art during the eras of American wars. Dozens of colorful war posters urge Americans to enlist, volunteer, buy bonds, and that "loose lips sink ships." In addition to posters, paintings and sketches also adorn the walls.

You could spend an entire day in the War Memorial Museum of Virginia, but the area has many more museums awaiting. One of the best is the U.S. Army Transportation Museum, located in Fort Eustis in Newport News.

The museum examines more than 200 years of Army transportation history, with indoor and outdoor displays that are often awe-inspiring. They range from miniature models to huge actual vehicles, aircraft, trains, jeeps, and marine craft from yesterday, today, and tomorrow.

One of the museum's first highlights is a film that relates the history of the Army's Transportation Corps and opens with a dramatic rising chorus of roaring engines and whirling blades. Visitors can feel and see the drama of moving soldiers and equipment in war and peace, from the "Red Ball Express" of World War II and the armored vehicles used in the jungles of Vietnam to the air-cushioned vehicles, cybernetic walking machines, and "flying jeeps" of today.

Outside, visitors can continue to explore the world of the Army in motion. Dozens of vehicles of all sorts are displayed, including the Army's largest helicopter, the *Flying Crane;* the *Caribou,* famed aircraft of the Army Parachute Team, the Golden Knights; the first helicopter to land at the South Pole; and a vertical take-off and landing aircraft.

If all of these vehicles make you want to go for a ride, head out for a Newport News Harbor Cruise. The cruise leaves from Wharton's Wharf and features a tour around Hampton Roads Harbor. Military buffs will enjoy a unique look at bustling Newport News Shipyard, where the giant aircraft carriers and submarines are being built.

Then the tour boat heads across to the Norfolk Naval Base for a look at the sleek nuclear submarines, carriers, cruisers, and support and supply vessels from around the world. The two-hour trip includes an interesting narration.

After the ride, there's still much more military history to explore. One fascinating possibility is the Casemate Museum on Fort Monroe. Sometimes called the "Gibraltar of the Chesapeake Bay," it is the largest stone fort ever built in the country and is the only moat-encircled fort still used by the Army. Construction of the fort began in 1819 and was not completed until 1934.

The Casemate Museum opened in 1951 to display the cell in which Jefferson Davis, the president of the Confederacy, was imprisoned after the Civil War. The museum has since been expanded to depict the history of Fort Monroe and the Coast Artillery Corps. The exhibits are located in the low-ceilinged casemates (small rooms from which guns are fired through narrow windows) designed to house seacoast artillery and include weapons, uniforms, models, drawings, and old living quarters.

The entire area has played a vital role in America's military past and today's active military presence, and its many museums seem to indicate it will continue to do so.

Specifically: For further information about the Hampton/ Newport News area, contact the Newport News Tourism Development Office, 50 Shoe Lane, Newport News, VA 23606, 804-594-7475 or 800-333-7787 or the Hampton Department of Conventions and Tourism, 2 Eaton Street, Hampton, VA 23669, 804-722-1222 or 800-487-8778.

25 Presidential Weekends

Virginia is often called "The Mother of Presidents." Virginians point with pride to the state's role as birthplace of more U.S. presidents – eight – than any other state. And that means a presidential weekend can include glimpses into the lives of George Washington, Thomas Jefferson, James Madison, James Monroe, William Henry Harrison, John Tyler, Zachary Taylor, and Woodrow Wilson.

Today, ten homes that these presidents once resided in still stand, and all but one are open to visitors. On any weekend, visitors can learn more about the men who led the country by seeing where and how they lived.

Mount Vernon, the home and burial place of George Washington, on the banks of the Potomac River, is one of America's most visited historic sites. Washington spent part of his youth on the property, in northern Virginia near Alexandria. Visitors can experience everything from the brightly painted walls the Washingtons preferred to the thirty acres of grounds and gardens, which remain substantially as the "father of our country" designed and left them.

To the south, in Westmoreland County on Virginia's Northern Neck, is the George Washington Birthplace National Monument. The original house, in which Washington was born in 1732, burned in 1779. Today, a colonial-style Memorial House, with furnishings representing the simple lifestyle of Washington's parents, stands on the site. In addition, a farm, kitchen, and workshop area with period-dressed guides help show how life was conducted on a typical plantation of the time.

Sherwood Forest, owned by Presidents William Henry Harrison and John Tyler, is located in Charles City, between

Williamsburg and Richmond (see Chapter 8). At 300 feet, the white-clapboard house is the longest frame house in America. Extensive boxwoods and English ivy frame Berkeley Plantation on the banks of the James River (see Chapter 8), the birthplace of the nation's ninth president, William Henry Harrison. It was also the ancestral home of the twenty-third president, Benjamin Harrison.

Near Lynchburg, weekend travelers who want to "get away from it all" can see Thomas Jefferson's getaway, Poplar Forest, the Palladian-style villa he designed and built primarily to serve as his retreat from the public.

North of Lynchburg, in the Shenandoah Valley city of Staunton, is the Woodrow Wilson Birthplace. Rare artifacts, photographs, and family and personal possessions of the Wilson family fill the house. In addition to guided tours of the house, visitors can explore the Woodrow Wilson Museum's seven exhibit galleries and view the Pierce-Arrow limousine that carried Wilson at his inaugural.

Less than an hour east of Staunton, set on a mountaintop in Albemarle County overlooking Charlottesville, is Thomas Jefferson's beloved Monticello (see Chapter 10). Jefferson designed and oversaw construction of his home over a period of forty years.

In 1739, James Monroe and his family moved into their Charlottesville "cabin castle," adjacent to Jefferson's Monticello. Jefferson chose the house site, had a hand in the purchase for his good friend, and planted the orchards at what is now known as Ash Lawn/Highland. Today, visitors to the estate can see the fifth president's original possessions in period-style room settings and explore a boxwood garden and a 535-acre working farm.

Northeast of Charlottesville, near Gordonsville, is the

birthplace of the twelfth president, Zachary Taylor. Although Montebello is not open to the public, a roadside marker on US 33 designates his birthplace.

James Madison, the fourth president and "father of the Constitution," lived at Montpelier in Orange County from infancy until his death in 1836. Visitors to Montpelier can take shuttle-bus tours of the property and cemetery and then visit the mansion where Madison and his wife, Dolly, entertained lavishly and frequently.

Near Leesburg, in northern Virginia, is Oak Hill, the home in later years of James Monroe, the man who held more political offices than any other president. The house, open to the public by appointment only, was designed by Thomas Jefferson. The name came from the sapling oaks – sent as gifts from each state – planted under Monroe's supervision.

Virginia's presidential legacy is large enough to keep visitors busy for many weekends. From Washington to Wilson, Virginia was (and is) for presidents and presidential weekends.

Specifically: For further information, contact: Mount Vernon, 703-780-2000; George Washington Birthplace National Monument, 804-224-1732; Sherwood Forest, 804-829-5377; Berkeley Plantation, 804-829-6018; Poplar Forest, 804-525-1806; Woodrow Wilson's Birthplace, 703-885-0897; Monticello, 804-295-8181; Ash Lawn/Highland, 804-293-9539; Montebello (not open to the public); Montpelier, 703-672-2728; and Oak Hill, 703-777-1246.

26 Theme Park Fun

Virginia's family fun centers offer adults and children a great way to spend a weekend day. Along with roller coasters and water slides, Busch Gardens, Water Country USA, Paramount's Kings Dominion, and Ocean Breeze Amusement Park also pay tribute to Old Europe and Hollywood movies, miniature sports, great gardens, shopper's delights, and tasty food.

For thrill-seekers, roller coaster fun comes in all varieties. At Paramount's Kings Dominion, just north of Richmond, you can try six different coasters. The park's newest wooden roller coaster, The Hurler, catapults riders at fifty miles per hour through the make-believe world of Wayne Campbell and Garth Algar, characters made famous in two Paramount movies, *Wayne's World* and *Wayne's World 2*.

For the less daring, Kings Dominion brings the world of Hollywood to Virginia. Movie fans will enjoy Paramount's re-created movie sets and highlights of film history and memorabilia from popular Paramount productions. Park visitors can learn about the "magic of the movies" back-stage or relax in an air-conditioned theater and take in live stage or ice-skating shows. For the same admission price, visitors can enjoy the bonus of Paramount's Hurricane Reef, an aquatic park with fifteen water slides. For an additional fee, visitors can often stay for special concerts by big-name performers.

Busch Gardens Williamsburg offers three roller coasters, including the German-designed Drachen Fire. One of the world's largest and most unusual roller coasters, Drachen Fire sends riders charging through looping corkscrews and other twists and turns, turning upside down eight times and

Take a ride on the wild side at Busch Gardens

producing a feeling of weightlessness. Survivors of the hair-raising ride can cool down on the Loch Ness Monster coaster, with speeds up to seventy miles per hour.

Busch Gardens visitors can also soak up the atmosphere of seventeenth-century life in nine re-created European hamlets that cover the rolling hills of the 360-acre park. Nearby, a narrated, self-guided brewery tour shows brands of America's most popular beers being made and includes tasting stops at the Anheuser-Busch Hospitality Center.

Water Country USA is just ten minutes from Busch Gardens. This park's chutes, tubes, pools, falls, waves, and slides make it the largest water park in the state. Surfer's Bay, a giant, heated, open-air water pool, is great for wading, swimming, or riding four-foot waves. For less active water pursuits, the park's Rambling River ride takes visitors floating through woodlands. The U.S. High Diving Team performers also offer entertainment.

Ocean Breeze Amusement Park, a multifaceted theme park, is just a short drive away in Virginia Beach. In the Strike Zone section of the park, major league–style batting cages challenge batters with fast balls, curve balls, and other surprises. Licensed drivers can test their racing skills at Motorworld's Formula One Grand Prix track. At Shipwreck Golf, young and old alike can experience the challenge of putting through caves, waterfalls, and other obstacles.

Whatever weekend thrills you desire, there's fun for everyone at Virginia's theme parks.

Specifically: For further information, contact: Paramount's Kings Dominion, 804-876-5000; Busch Gardens Williamsburg, 804-253-3350; Water Country USA, 804-229-9300 or 800-343-SWIM; and Ocean Breeze Amusement Park, 804-422-4444 or 800-678-9453.

Fall

27 A Leaf Peeper's Weekend

"Virginia puts on her prettiest colors to greet the seasons.
In the fall, the colors of the leaves are lemon yellow,
pumpkin gold, watermelon red, rusty oak,
vermillion maple, burnt orange, and dusty green,
and no two trees are the same."
    – Virginia native Earl Hamner Jr.

Fall comes early and stays late in Virginia. The state is ideal for a weekend of colorful leaf-peeping.

As early as late September, Virginia's northwestern and southwestern mountain regions shimmer with the changing colors of maple, hickory, dogwood, and oak trees. In mid-October, color cascades from the Blue Ridge and Allegheny mountains, across the Shenandoah Valley, to the foothills of central Virginia. From mid-October through mid-November, Hampton Roads/Tidewater and the Eastern Shore are in full color.

In the southwest Blue Ridge Highlands, the Appalachian Trail and the Daniel Boone Wilderness Trail provide hiking enthusiasts with colorful challenges in Virginia's Allegheny Mountains. The Blue Ridge Parkway (see Chapter 28) stretches from Waynesboro into North Carolina through the Blue

Ridge Mountains. At Waynesboro, it joins the 105-mile Skyline Drive (see Chapter 28), which rides the top of Shenandoah National Park.

Central Virginia boasts rolling hills and rich farmland, in addition to the state capital. The colors of fall accent numerous Civil War reenactments and equestrian events in the region.

Northern Virginia's George Washington Parkway, leading from Mount Vernon to the monuments of nearby Washington, D.C., is ideal for walking, cycling, or driving tours. Historic districts, such as those in Fredericksburg, Alexandria, Middleburg, and Waterford, are particularly interesting because special care has been taken to preserve and maintain the feel of an era.

In the Hampton Roads/Tidewater area and on Virginia's Eastern Shore, fall color changes occur first along tidal rivers and streams leading to the Atlantic Ocean and Chesapeake Bay. Seafood festivals and the reenactment of America's first Thanksgiving at Berkeley Plantation allow additional opportunities to enjoy the season.

Leaf-peeping weekenders can combine spectacular fall foliage viewing with accommodations at resorts, bed-and-breakfasts, and country inns throughout the state for a relaxing, colorful weekend.

Specifically: For information on fall foliage along the Skyline Drive in Shenandoah National Park, call 703-999-2266 or 800-354-4595 for a recorded message or 703-999-2243 to speak with someone directly. For information on fall foliage along the Blue Ridge Parkway, call 704-298-0398 for a recorded message or 703-857-2213 or 704-298-0192 to speak with someone directly.

28 Falling for the Skyline Drive and the Blue Ridge Parkway

The Skyline Drive and Blue Ridge Parkway combine to make one of the nation's most beautiful and intriguing stretches of road. The fall colors provide a perfect time to spend a weekend enjoying sections of the drive and enjoying the wide variety of accommodations and dining options along the way.

The Skyline Drive runs from the north entrance at Front Royal for 105 miles to the south Rockfish entrance. The speed limit is a leisurely thirty-five miles per hour, and there are excellent signs, concrete mile markers, and rock fence guardrails all along the way.

Fall attracts lots of leaf-peepers, but the view is well worth any hassles caused by crowding. Just be sure to plan weekend accommodations in advance. The colors typically reach their peak in mid-October, but a quick phone call will help ensure that you don't miss a thing when you visit.

The natural beauty of the drive begins almost at the start of the drive, just south of Front Royal, where you pay a few bucks per car for the privilege of driving along one of the nation's most colorful roads anytime of year. The entrance station is staffed by friendly National Park Service personnel who can answer questions and provide specific recommendations.

The entire drive is blessed with beautiful overlooks, and drivers are frequently drawn off the road for some spectacular views. To make the most of the trip, stop often to admire the fall colors or take in some great hiking and picnicking.

At milepost 4.6, you can stop at the Dickey Ridge visitors center for specific ideas for your trip, for ranger talks and walks, for hiking recommendations, and to find out what's open and closed. This major facility features exhibits on Skyline Drive services and activities, an interesting sales outlet, park rangers to answer questions, a self-guided nature trail, and much more.

About a mile past Thornton Gap is Marys Rock Tunnel. Built in 1932, this car tunnel passes through 600 feet of rock with a thirteen-foot clearance. It makes for some fun picture possibilities from both ends, with fall colors as your background.

Skyland (mileposts 41.7 and 42.5), one of the busiest spots on the drive, is another great place to head for information, food, or for a place to spend the night. At 3,680 feet, it is the highest point on the drive.

Naturalist George Freeman Pollock, a major backer of building the park, built Skyland resort in the 1890s. It has developed into a popular target for many Skyline Drive visitors. One feature of the resort is the Appalachian Trail, which runs right through the grounds. Look for the Appalachian Trail Overlook around milepost 100. The famed Appalachian Trail is a 2,100-mile hiking "path" along the ridge of the Appalachian Mountains, stretching from Maine to Georgia. It runs through fourteen states, and the Virginia section, at 534 miles long, is the longest stretch.

The Skyland Lodge features large rooms for the night, with terraces overlooking the Shenandoah Valley. Skyland also has several rustic cabins for rent, as well as a spacious restaurant with great views.

The Big Meadows area (mileposts 51 and 51.2) has one of the more unusual sights along the Skyland Drive. Park managers have intentionally maintained the area as it was before it became a park, when the land was overused. As a result, visitors still see an open area, with little vegetation.

This busy area is also a great place for a short or long stop. The best place to start your visit is at the Byrd visitors center, where rangers can help with plans, information, hikes, and much more. The wayside facilities nearby include a coffee shop, camp store, gift shop, and service station. (There aren't too many on the Skyline Drive, so watch your tank!) The Big Meadows Lodge features spacious rooms and cabins overlooking the Shenandoah Valley. Camping (no trailer hookups) is very popular at Big Meadows, so call ahead for reservations. There is also a casually rustic restaurant with great views.

Lewis Mountain (milepost 57.4) provides another place to eat, sleep, and be merry in the great outdoors. It offers camping and cabin accommodations, as well as a camp store, picnicking, and campground programs.

The drive continues southward, meandering past incredible vistas and views. You lose track of which overlook had the most spectacular fall colors, but that's a nice problem to have.

Milepost 105.4 marks the end of the Skyline Drive, but the Blue Ridge Parkway is straight ahead, making this weekend drive duo one of the best "no-turn" fall drives.

Since its inception, the Blue Ridge Parkway has been called America's favorite drive. It was authorized in the 1930s as a Depression-era public works project, but was a half-century in the making. It was the nation's first (and ultimately the longest) rural parkway. It connects the Shenandoah National Park in Virginia (the Skyline Drive) with the Great Smoky Mountains National Park in North Carolina. Virginia's portion features about 215 miles of pure fall weekend pleasure.

The first major stop is a good example of what the drive has to offer. The Humpback Rocks visitors center (milepost 59.3) is often the first taste of the Blue Ridge Parkway for southbound drivers and it's a breath-stopper.

The system of visitor centers, camping facilities, and

concessions on the parkway is excellent, with services varying with the season. The various stopping points are great places to get maps, ask questions, and learn about campfire talks, nature walks, slide programs, and much more.

The Humpback Rocks area features an interesting self-guided tour through a reconstructed mountain farmstead. The short, but steep, hike up to Humpback Rocks (at milepost 6.1) is well worth the heavy breathing for a breathtaking view of the area. And it's really only three-quarters of a mile to the top.

Just down the road is the turnoff for Wintergreen Resort (see Chapter 2), a thriving four-season mountain resort offering skiing, golf, tennis, swimming pools, an equestrian center, an indoor spa, and lots of places to spend the night and enjoy a good meal. It's a great place to stay if you got a late start on the parkway.

Country-inn fans will want to head for the Trillium House, where Ed and Betty Dinwiddie have run a wonderful inn since 1983. They offer twelve quaint guest rooms, a spacious "great room" (perfect for après-ski and post-hike chats), a popular TV room, and an interesting family library. Meals, creatively prepared by chef Ellen English, are served in the dining room (with wonderful views of the mountain and golf course). The breakfasts are huge and the weekend meals are worth a drive down (or up) the mountain.

Back on the Blue Ridge Parkway, the fall colors begin in earnest, but if you stopped at every awe-inspiring view, you'd never make it to the North Carolina border.

Between mileposts 58 and 64, the Otter Creek runs down the Blue Ridge, following the road to the James River. Otters don't play along the creek anymore, but lots of people do. This section of the drive features a year-round campground, a visitors center, a self-guided nature trail, a restored lock and canal system, a restaurant, a gift shop, and the lowest elevation on the entire parkway (649 feet).

Peaks of Otter (see Chapter 38) is next and it's one of the highlights of a drive along the Blue Ridge Parkway. Make time to stop for a few hours, the night, or a few days. Peaks of Otter Lodge is a great place to enjoy the life along the parkway. Its simple rooms overlook Abbott Lake and are priced quite moderately. The restaurant features great dining with a special buffet from the sea on Friday nights and a country dinner buffet on Sunday nights.

The parkway continues south and the spectacular views roll by continuously.

Like Peaks of Otter, the Rocky Knob area is a highlight of the drive. The visitors center has some spectacular hiking recommendations and information about accommodations in the Rocky Knob Cabins, which offer a unique way to spend the night in the Blue Ridge Mountains.

Mabry Mill is just down the road. This often-photographed water-powered mill was operated by E.B. Mabry from 1910 to 1935. The self-guided walking tour includes his gristmill, sawmill, blacksmith shop, and other outdoor exhibits. In the fall and summer, visitors will often find staff members demonstrating a variety of old-time skills.

The rest of the Virginia portion of the Blue Ridge Parkway is steeped in views, gaps, and history. For views, pull off at the Groundhog Mountain Parking Overlook and head for its observation tower, which resembles an old tobacco barn. For gaps, try the quaint town of Fancy Gap. It's a perfect ending to this fancy fall drive.

Specifically: For information about the Skyline Drive, contact the Shenandoah National Park at Route 4, Box 348, Luray, VA 22835, 703-999-2266 (recorded message);

800-999-4714 or 703-743-5108 (lodging reservations); 800-732-0911 (emergencies only). For general information about the Blue Ridge Parkway, contact 2551 Mountain Road, Vinton, VA 24179, 703-982-6213. For information about Wintergreen Resort, call 804-325-2300. For accommodations or dining reservations at the Trillium House, call 804-325-9126 or 800-325-9126. For accommodations and dining reservations at Peaks of Otter Lodge, call 703-586-1081. For information about the Appalachian Trail contact the Appalachian Trail Conference at P.O. Box 807, Harpers Ferry, WV 25425, 304-535-6331.

29 Oh, Shenandoah
Shenandoah Valley

"Oh, Shenandoah, I long to see you . . ."
– "Shenandoah" lyrics

Getting there can still be half the fun for a weekend away. Plane travel has made globe-trotting trendy, but cars are still a better way to enjoy the true treasures of travel. And for many people, one treasure is a fall foliage weekend of driving in the Shenandoah Valley. The location and road system make the drive a big part of the fun.

Made famous by song and history, Shenandoah is an Indian word, meaning "daughter of the stars." This picturesque area is flanked by wooded hills and mountains ranging in elevation from 3,000 to 5,000 feet. The valley is generally ten to twenty miles wide and features many small towns and lots of rolling farmland.

Throughout the area, fall tourists find lots to see and do. There's incredible scenery, historical sites, world-famous caverns, renowned wineries, antique shopping, and a full array of tourism services. Accommodations range from quaint bed and breakfasts to large resorts. Drivers can use one place in the Shenandoah Valley as a base for exploration or easily cover the entire length for a complete overview.

"Our area is perfect for the weekend," says Andy Dawson, head of the Shenandoah Valley Travel Association. "The places and the people make this a very special destination."

Winchester offers an ideal place to start a Shenandoah Valley weekend. The town is blessed with both Civil War history and a thriving apple industry. Many Shenandoah Valley visitors make a beeline to Winchester on the first weekend in May for the Apple Blossom Festival. This annual event features parades, fairs, and special events.

Just a few miles down US 11, the little town of Middletown has enough to keep you busy for the entire weekend. Highlights include spending the night or dining at the historic Wayside Inn, catching a production at Wayside Theatre, or snacking the tasty chips at Route 11 Potato Chips.

The next stop along the road is Strasburg, rightfully known as "The Antique Capital of the Blue Ridge." The Strasburg Emporium answers the wishes of any antique shopper, with almost 100 dealers under one roof. Historic Strasburg also features several interesting museums, the Civil War site of Hupps Hill Battlefield Park and Study Center, and the Hotel Strasburg, where you can stay for the night or at least enjoy the fine dining and the historic old inn setting.

In Woodstock, look for the oldest county courthouse in use west of the Blue Ridge Mountains, dating from 1792. Overnighters should head for the Inn at Narrow Passage. This log inn overlooking the Shenandoah River has been welcoming travelers since the early 1740s. It has been a haven for settlers on the Virginia frontier and was a stagecoach inn on the old Valley Turnpike, as well as serving as the 1862 headquarters for Stonewall Jackson during the Valley Campaign.

Ellen and Ed Markel now welcome visitors to this quaint bed and breakfast. The inn is furnished in antiques and handcrafted colonial reproductions and has comfortable rooms with private or shared baths. Some of the rooms have romantic and rustic wood-burning fireplaces and canopy beds. The Markels love to share the Shenandoah Valley with fall visitors.

Heading south out of Woodstock, take the turnoff to Shenandoah Vineyards, which is a right on State 605 and then a left on State 686. Owner Emma Randel has made Shenandoah Vineyards one of the state's most renowned wineries (see Chapter 32).

Just south of Mount Jackson, look for the turn to the covered bridge on State 720. This is the longest covered bridge of the nine remaining in Virginia and is the last crossing the Shenandoah River.

If you've never visited underground caverns, the Shenandoah Valley is the place to start. If you've seen some caverns, go anyway. Shenandoah Caverns is convenient to US 11 and provides an ideal introduction to the underbelly of the Shenandoah Valley (it's even pretty underground).

Shenandoah Caverns surprises many people with its sheer beauty, great tours, and stunning lighting. You descend by elevator to Bacon Hall, which was once featured in *National Geographic*. The formations here look incredibly like strips of bacon, and this sets the tone for the rest of the unique mile-long walking tour.

The New Market area played a key role in the Civil War. New Market Battlefield Park memorializes the brave charge of cadets from the Virginia Military Institute on May 15, 1864. Visitors here can enjoy extensive historical exhibits and a tour of the battlefield.

The Shenandoah Valley Travel Association information center is also located in New Market, just off I-81. Open 9:00 A.M. to 5:00 P.M. daily, this is a great place to stock up on information and literature about the entire Shenandoah Valley.

The drive from New Market down to Harrisonburg passes through lots of farmland and history. Harrisonburg is the home of James Madison University, Eastern Mennonite College, and the headquarters for the George Washington National Forest (the mountainous western boundary of the Shenandoah Valley). Be sure to save time for a night (or at least a meal) at Joshua Wilton House downtown.

Scenic Staunton is one of the valley's most varied stops.

The hilly town offers great shopping, dining, and accommodation options, and for a dollop of history, the Woodrow Wilson Birthplace gives a great overview of the life and times of the twenty-eighth president of the U.S. Three great places to stay are the Belle Grae Inn, Sampson Eagon Inn, and Frederick House.

The countryside surrounding Staunton also provides opportunities for outings, including the Museum of American Frontier Culture, with its fascinating eighteenth- and nineteenth-century working farms.

Farther down the valley, the town of Lexington lures weekend travelers with lots of history and modern-day attractions. A nineteenth-century college town, Lexington is home to the Virginia Military Institute and Washington and Lee University. Be sure to visit both campuses and the historic downtown. There are several nice bed-and-breakfast possibilities (contact Historic Country Inns of Lexington or one of many bed and breakfasts recommended by the tourist office), as well as casual college-style dining at Spanky's.

Just south of Lexington is Natural Bridge, one of the seven natural wonders of the world. This 215-foot-high stone arch was carved by water over countless centuries and is one of the Shenandoah Valley's most famous sites.

Roanoke is the valley's largest city and marks the southern end of this famous region. It is known as the "Capital of the Blue Ridge" and features a city market in operation since 1878 and Center on the Square, a regional center for art, history, science, and culture. The Roanoke Valley Historical Society gives an excellent overview of the area, which mirrored the development of the entire Shenandoah Valley in many ways. The Patrick Henry Hotel and Mary Bladon House are two great places to stay right in town.

Although Roanoke is the official end of the Shenandoah

Cutting hay at the Museum of American Frontier Culture

Valley, there is much more farther south on I-81 or US 11 if you want to see more of southwest Virginia (see Chapter 30) or you're looking for an unusual weekend in the Old Dominion.

Specifically: For further information, contact the Shenandoah Valley Travel Association, P.O. Box 1040, Dept. STS, New Market, VA 22844, 703-740-3132. Ask about its excellent Shenandoah Valley Travel Guide and Calendar of Events.

For a weekend in the Shenandoah Valley, some other helpful contacts include: Winchester Chamber of Commerce, 703-662-4135 or 800-662-1360; Wayside Inn, 703-869-1797; Wayside Theatre, 703-869-1776; Route 11 Potato Chips, 703-869-0104; Strasburg Emporium, 703-465-3711; Hupps Hill Battlefield Park and Study Center, 703-465-5884; Hotel Strasburg, 703-465-9191; Inn at Narrow Passage, Woodstock, 703-459-8000; Shenandoah Vineyards, 703-984-8669; Shenandoah Caverns, 703-477-3115; New Market Battlefield Historical Park, 703-740-3101; Joshua Wilton House, 703-434-4464; Staunton/Augusta Travel Information Center, 703-332-3865; Belle Grae Inn, 703-886-5151; Sampson Eagon Inn, 703-886-2200; Frederick House, 800-334-5575; Museum of American Frontier Culture, 703-332-7850; Lexington Visitors Bureau and visitors center, 703-463-3777; Historic Country Inns of Lexington, 703-463-2044; Spanky's, 703-463-3338; Natural Bridge, 703-291-2121 or 800-533-1410; Roanoke Valley Visitor Information Center, 703-345-8622; Patrick Henry Hotel, 703-345-8811; and Mary Bladon House, 703-344-5361.

30 The Secrets of Southwest Virginia

Southwest Virginia often plays second fiddle to the rest of the Old Dominion, but only because of the long drive it typically takes to reach the area. Once there, weekend explorers find a beautiful and peaceful region with interesting things to see and do.

Abingdon serves as the beginning of an exploration of southwest Virginia along US 58. Take US 11 or I-81 south toward Bristol, get on US 58 west, and head into another world. Make Abingdon your southwest Virginia base and try to stay at the Martha Washington Inn (see Chapter 44).

The rolling countryside and sheer beauty begin almost immediately and the area is filled with history. Daniel Boone made his way through here in 1775 on the route from Big Moccasin Gap all the way to Boonsboro, Kentucky. The scenic road, which follows an original Indian path, was known as the Wilderness Road, and it has produced generations of proud mountain folk.

You can take a closer look at local life by taking US 58/County 421 west to Hiltons and then turning north onto County 614. Up in Maces Spring, traditional mountain music fans flock to the Carter Family Memorial Music Center.

The original Carter family members (Maybelle, A. P., and Sara) were discovered by a talent scout in 1927. Country-music scholar Douglas B. Green wrote, "The Carters' music was as haunting, mournful and beautiful as the Appalachians from which it came." They went on to record 300 songs, including "My Clinch Mountain Home," "Keep on the Sunny Side," and "Wildwood Flower."

A. P. and Sara's daughter, Janette, started this intriguing memorial in the shadow of Clinch Mountain. It includes a Carter Family Museum and the Carter Family Fold, where traditional and bluegrass music are played every Saturday night. There's also a huge festival in August to commemorate the first recording the Carter family made. It's worth the detour on a Saturday, but be sure to call first.

After skirting around Weber City and Gate City, US 58/County 421 heads for Natural Tunnel State Park and a glimpse of Mother Nature's power. Just outside of Duffield, Natural Tunnel is a huge underground tunnel formed more than one million years ago when limestone and dolomitic bedrock was slowly eroded by groundwater that contained carbonic acid. Later, the flow of Stock Creek enlarged the opening to its present height of more than 400 feet. The new visitors center is a great place to go for further information about the "Eighth Wonder of the World."

One can't-miss diversion along this scenic road is Big Stone Gap. Just fifteen miles north on US 23, Big Stone Gap offers an entire day of interesting possibilities. Check out the tourist information office as you head into town—it's in a restored 1891 Pullman Company train car.

Big Stone Gap is famed for its outdoor presentation of the drama, "Trail of the Lonesome Pine." The play tells the love story of a Virginia mountain girl and a handsome young mining engineer from the east. It depicts the great coal-and-iron ore days of the region, as well as the proud people, and makes effective use of both the powerful story and memorable setting.

Next door to the small outdoor theater on Clinton Avenue is the Jane Tolliver House and Craft Shop. The heroine of the drama actually lived in this pretty house while attending school nearby. The home now features restored nineteenth-century furnishings and a great collection of local crafts.

In the center of Big Stone Gap, the John Fox Jr. Museum

serves as a memorial to the author of *Trail of the Lonesome Pine*. His book was the first novel to sell a million copies in the country. The interesting house was built in 1888 and contains furnishings and memorabilia from the Fox family.

Modern-day weekend explorers of the region shouldn't miss the Southwest Virginia Museum on Wood Avenue, housed in a beautiful home built of local limestone and sandstone. This intriguing state-run museum depicts the pioneer life and development of Big Stone Gap and the region. The informative displays and artifacts provide a unique insight into the history of the area, and visitors depart with a new appreciation of southwest Virginia.

Other interesting stops in Big Stone Gap include the Harry W. Meador Jr. Coal Museum, the Victorian homes of Poplar Hill, and the memorial at Miner's Park (the town is known as the "Gateway to the Coalfields"). With all of this history packed into such a small town, Big Stone Gap is definitely worth the small diversion from the main roads. If you have time for a meal, head for the Mutual Pharmacy on Wood Avenue. This typical small-town store and eatery is a wonderful way to meet the locals.

After Duffield, US 58 rolls southwest the last fifty-four miles to Cumberland Gap. Small towns like Dot, Rose Hill, and Ewing sit in the shadows of Powell Mountain and later, Cumberland Mountain. But Cumberland Gap is the draw, just as it has been for centuries.

Daniel Boone came to the area in 1775 with thirty men and marked out the Wilderness Trail from Cumberland Gap into Kentucky. That began the mass immigration through the gap, with 12,000 people crossing into the new territory by the end of the Revolutionary War. By the time Kentucky was admitted to the Union in 1792, another 100,000 had crossed through the gap.

Today, Cumberland Gap, situated at the convergence of Virginia, Kentucky, and Tennessee, is a major tourist attraction and well worth the drive. To begin your visit, it's actually best to head out of Virginia for a brief time for a stop at the Cumberland Gap visitors center and Park Headquarters in Middlesboro, Kentucky.

Highlights of a drive to and around the Cumberland Gap National Historical Park include more than fifty miles of hiking trails, excellent camping and picnicking facilities, the Hensley Settlement on Brush Mountain, and simply incredible views. And if you take the switch-back Pinnacle Road up to Pinnacle Overlook, you'll be rewarded with a 2,440-foot view over three states.

Cumberland Gap marks the end of the Virginia portion of the Wilderness Road, but it was only the beginning for settlers heading west. Modern-day drivers can head back east along US 58 to Abingdon or they can make a loop by taking US Alternate 58 from Jonesville through Pennington Gap, Big Stone Gap (see earlier description), and Norton.

This pretty drive meanders through the Jefferson National Forest, back to Abingdon, and through Big Stone Gap. In nearby Norton, craft-shoppers will love the Appalachian Peddler, a Victorian home now packed with handcrafted Appalachian products. View-shoppers should head for Flag Rock or High Knob to enjoy some of Virginia's best scenery before heading back to Abingdon.

Specifically: For further information about a weekend in southwest Virginia, contact: Abingdon Convention and Visitors Bureau, 703-676-2282; Martha Washington Inn,

703-628-3161 or 800-533-1014; Carter Family Memorial Music Center, 703-386-9480; Natural Tunnel State Park, 703-940-2674; Car 101 Tourist Information Center, 703-523-2060; Trail of the Lonesome Pine Outdoor Drama, 703-523-1235; Southwest Virginia Museum, 703-523-1322; Cumberland Gap National Historical Park, 606-248-2817; and Appalachian Peddler, 703-679-5927.

31 Good Night, John-Boy
Schuyler

"You know, Thomas Wolfe couldn't 'go home again'
because of the things he'd written. But I can go home,
and do, because I've written with affection
about our life together."
  — Earl Hamner Jr.

A visit to the Waltons Mountain Museum is like a trip to the country to see old family friends. You feel as if you've known the Walton family all of your life, and you're just now getting to see where they've lived for so long.

You can almost hear one of the Walton kids calling, "Good night, John-Boy," from down the hall. This museum is just one of those places that gives you a warm, fuzzy, familial feeling as soon as you step inside.

The Waltons were everyone's TV family for more than a decade. Winner of thirteen Emmys and many other awards, the television series portrayed the independence, sturdiness, and closeness of Blue Ridge Mountain people through the story of one memorable family.

The series traced the Waltons through good times and bad, showing how they lived in the years before World War II. Families across America came to know and love John-Boy, Mary Ellen, Olivia, John, Grandpa and Grandma Walton, Ike Godsey, and many other characters.

The stories were based on the experiences of the show's creator, Earl Hamner Jr., who was born in Schuyler on July 10, 1923, the oldest of eight children. A writer by nature, he faithfully recorded his childhood in journals that were to become the basis for many of his later works.

After attending college in Virginia, Hamner began his career writing for radio in Cincinnati and New York before

114

migrating to Hollywood. There, he developed a successful career writing novels and writing scripts for films and television.

His novel *Spencer's Mountain*, based on his childhood in Schuyler, was turned into a hit movie in 1963. In 1971, his Christmas teleplay, "The Homecoming," led to the creation of "The Waltons," one of the most successful and enduring television shows in history.

The interest in the show and family is so great that people still flock to the Schuyler area as a Waltons mecca. With the museum, they have an even better reason to head for this town, nestled in the foothills of Nelson County.

The Walton's Mountain Museum was created to support the non-profit Schuyler Community Center, which provides recreational, cultural, and other services to the people of the Schuyler area. The center and museum have brought the community together in ways rarely seen in today's society.

The museum was a labor of love for hundreds of Schuyler volunteers. "The people of Schuyler made this happen," says founder Bill Luhrs. It is located in the community center, which was once the school Earl Hamner attended with his seven brothers and sisters.

The Walton's Mountain Museum features professionally prepared and presented re-creations of sets from the show, designed by architect Robert Brent Hall, a Schuyler native now based in Charlottesville. John-Boy's room is the first exhibit, found down a long hallway of fascinating Hamner and Walton memorabilia.

The bedroom re-creation includes a rocking chair for reading, an old writing desk, and a typing table, all looking out over Schuyler. Locals say the town outside really hasn't changed much since John-Boy (Earl Hamner) was growing up just down the street (the Hamner house still stands).

The next room features a reproduction of Ike Godsey's store, with all sorts of period pieces. Visitors typically gravitate to Ike's counter, the phone, and the post-office boxes. The room also serves as the museum store and has local arts and crafts for sale.

The kitchen comes next, with a long wooden table and a big old stove. Walking by, you can just imagine the smells of country cooking. The warm living room follows, with comfortable chairs and old copies of *Grit* magazine dating back to the 1920s.

The museum has also opened a room where visitors can watch videotapes of interviews with former cast members and with Earl Hamner Jr., as well as episodes of the show. Who knows, maybe Earl or another Hamner family member will stop by for a visit.

Specifically: For more information, contact the Walton's Mountain Museum at P.O. Box 124, Schuyler, VA 22969, 804-831-2000. A trip to the museum can easily be combined with a weekend in Jefferson's Charlottesville (see Chapter 10).

32 Visiting Virginia's Vineyards

Virginia has a long wine history. Ideal soil and weather conditions have made the state's winemakers so successful that *The Wine Spectator* named Virginia "the most accomplished of America's emerging wine regions."

Winemaking in Virginia began in 1607, when the Jamestown settlers fermented native American grapes to make the first wines in the New World. In the 1700s, Thomas Jefferson introduced his native Virginians and the new nation to the European custom of taking wine with meals. He also tried growing the delicate European grape varietals in his Monticello vineyard. For his pioneering efforts, Jefferson is revered as the "father of American wine."

Up until the late 1850s, Virginia was a major wine-growing state and won international acclaim for claret wine produced in Charlottesville. However, Virginia's young vineyards suffered during the 1860s from the many Civil War battles fought on Virginia soil, and received another setback in the Prohibition era of the 1920s. After Prohibition ended, some Virginians, such as Paul Garrett and his Virginia Dare Company, tried to meet the demands of a once-strong national and international market. But while they had some success in forming wine-growers groups in the Monticello viticultural area, the years of prohibition had devastated the industry too much for it to recover quickly.

The modern wine-growing industry has learned from the pioneering efforts of Virginians, with new acreage being planted in northern Virginia and in other regions of the state. Virginia now has six specially designated growing regions, or viticultural areas: Monticello, Northern Neck George Washington Birthplace, Shenandoah Valley, Rocky Knob, Eastern Shore, and North Fork of the Roanoke.

Testing the new vintage

The number of farm wineries has grown from six in 1979 to more than forty-five today. With 130 commercial vineyards, Virginia now has more than 1,400 acres devoted to wine grapes, up from 286 acres in 1979. A visit to one or more vineyards, especially during the frequent and lively festivals they host, is the perfect way to spend a weekend in the Virginia countryside. Each winery has its own proud history to relate and its own distinctive product to taste.

Festivals are scheduled year-round, but many occur during October, which is Virginia Wine Month. The festivals feature craft shows, family picnics, music, outdoor activities, tastings, grape stompings, wine making, and much more. In addition, most vineyards operate tours, providing a first-hand look at the modern techniques that are making Virginia one of the finest wine-producing areas in the world, with a growing list of awards to prove it.

Virginia's vineyards and wineries are located throughout the state, but many are concentrated in the Shenandoah Valley, along the Blue Ridge Mountains, on the Charlottesville hillsides, and in northern Virginia. Visitors can just follow the grape logo highway signs to Virginia's many vineyards for a tasty weekend.

Specifically: For information about Virginia vineyards and festivals, contact the Virginia Wine Marketing Program through the Virginia Department of Agricultural and Consumer Services, P.O. Box 1163, Richmond, VA 23209, 804-786-0481 or 800-828-4637.

33 Sugar Tree Inn
Steeles Tavern

The trees of Virginia come alive each fall, and from a rocker on the front porch of the Sugar Tree Inn, you can sit back, relax, and admire the splendor. The colorful view, stretching forty miles across the Shenandoah Valley into the Allegheny Mountains, seems almost endless, and so do the weekend possibilities at the quaint Sugar Tree Inn, operated by innkeepers and hosts Sarah and Hal Davis.

Set on twenty-eight wooded acres a half mile high and less than a mile from the famed Blue Ridge Parkway, the Sugar Tree Inn provides both peace and solitude. You relax from the moment you arrive, picking a rocker on the broad front porch, hearing the leaves rustling in the wind, listening to the birds in the forest, and watching a mountain sunset as evening falls.

Inside, a beautiful lodge and guest rooms await visitors. Ancient hand-hewn beams and logs saved from historic Shenandoah Valley structures were used to construct the lodge, and a massive stone fireplace rises two stories to a skylit ceiling. Upstairs or on the grounds, every rustic room and suite offers chairs by the fire, comfortable beds with country quilts or comforters, and private baths. Some suites even boast whirlpool tubs, ceiling fans, VCRs, and separate sitting rooms.

Dinnertime is always a special time at the Sugar Tree Inn. Light evening fare is available to guests, by reservation, on Fridays and Saturdays. Haute country cuisine at the inn means quiet music, candlelight, and an ever-changing creative menu, with dishes such as Williamsburg peanut soup, Virginia chicken breast with country ham bread sauce, and Aunt Gertie's corn pudding.

In the morning, guests head to the glass-walled dining room, which seems to bring the fall colors inside. The breakfast features an endless array of meats, entrees, fruits, cereals, and breads.

During the day, there is much to explore in the fall (or almost anytime of year—they're open from April through November). The options include heading up to the Blue Ridge Parkway, hiking, biking, admiring waterfalls, shopping, wine-tasting, visiting the Natural Bridge, and touring the historic towns of Lexington and Staunton.

Specifically: Contact the Sugar Tree Inn at State 56, Steeles Tavern, VA 24476-9999, 703-377-2197.

34 Back to School

Virginia's college and university campuses are more than just places of study. They offer weekend travelers unusual museums, gardens, architectural gems, a wealth of history, and much more. And most of them welcome visitors with free walking tours and provide a wide variety of cultural events.

In northern Virginia, George Mason University in Fairfax is home to the Center for the Arts, which hosts dance, music, and theater performances from around the world. This modern big-city campus bustles with activities throughout the year.

Built on the site of a Civil War battleground overlooking Fredericksburg, Mary Washington College is located south of Fairfax off I-95. The college administers the James Monroe Law Office-Museum and Memorial Library and displays the Louis XVI desk where the fifth president wrote his famous doctrine in 1823.

Farther south, in Richmond, Virginia Commonwealth University presents student art exhibitions at its Anderson Gallery and dance performances in centers throughout the city. Two campus theaters—the Shafer Street Playhouse and the Raymond Hodges Theater—present student theatrical productions.

Union Theological Seminary's campus in Richmond is known for its distinctive red-brick Victorian Gothic buildings. One of them is the home of the largest of four gargoyles in Richmond, and another building is said to be haunted.

Twenty miles south, in Petersburg, is Virginia State University, the first fully state-supported liberal arts college for African Americans in the nation. An exhibit of artifacts of Petersburg's Black history is housed on campus, along with a fine collection of African art in the school's Meredith Art Gallery.

Williamsburg, an hour's drive east of Richmond, is home to the College of William and Mary, the nation's second-oldest institution of higher learning. The college recently celebrated its 300th anniversary.

On the campus of Christopher Newport University, southeast of Williamsburg in Newport News, an authentic Japanese tea house has been reconstructed by a Japanese company specializing in traditional building techniques. The architecture replicates the sixteenth-century Ennan Tea House in Kyoto, Japan. Tours are available by appointment.

Across the peninsula is Hampton University, founded in 1868 to educate freed slaves. The university also taught Native Americans from tribes throughout the country. Visitors to the Hampton Institute Museum, renowned for its collection of African, African-American, and Native American art, can see a beaded vest worn by Chief Geronimo, as well as Henry O. Tanner's famous painting *The Banjo Lesson*.

Nearby Norfolk is home to another predominantly African-American college, Norfolk State University (NSU). The NSU players stage four or five open-to-the-public theatrical productions each year. Another Norfolk school, Old Dominion University, offers a wide range of concerts, performances, and lectures throughout the year, which are open to the public.

Traveling west to Farmville, one can see where frightened young Longwood College students watched Gen. Robert E. Lee's army retreat at the end of the Civil War. Visitors can also view the rotunda (built in 1905), walk a fitness trail, or access information from around the world using Longwood's new, high-technology library.

Nearby Hampden-Sydney College, founded in 1776, is a National Historic Preservation district with a nationally registered arboretum featuring more than 300 different kinds of trees, plants, and flowers; a nineteenth-century herb garden; and an oak given as a sapling following the Virginia State Constitutional Convention in 1901.

Less than an hour away, in Lynchburg, Randolph-Macon Woman's College owns a distinctive collection of American art. Works by Georgia O'Keefe, Mary Cassatt, and Thomas Hart Benton can be found in hallways and offices throughout the campus and in the college's Maier Museum of Art.

North of Lynchburg, in the foothills of the Blue Ridge Mountains, is Sweet Briar College. This college for women has one of the prettiest campuses in the state.

Farther north, in Charlottesville, is the University of Virginia, founded by Thomas Jefferson and home to the Bayly Museum of Art. The university offers free guided tours every day of the classically designed lawn and rotunda.

Moving back up to the northwest portion of the state and traveling down I-81 through the Shenandoah Valley, the Harrisonburg area is home to three campuses offering sights for weekend visitors. Bentley, a twelve-foot boa constrictor, resides at the Life Science Museum at James Madison University, along with a collection of seashells; live fish, insects, mammals, and reptiles; and mounted birds.

At another Harrisonburg school, Eastern Mennonite College and Seminary, a stuffed two-headed calf born in Rockingham County is displayed at the college's D. R. Hostettler Museum of Natural History, along with a collection of mounted animals of America and Africa.

Nearby is Bridgewater College, Virginia's first coeducational institution of higher learning. The school's Reuel B.

Pritchett Museum displays the 800-year-old remains of an Indian child and a three-volume 1482 Venice Bible.

The 150-year-old Mary Baldwin College is located south of Harrisonburg in the Shenandoah Valley city of Staunton. The pretty campus, once led by President Woodrow Wilson's father, is across the street from the Woodrow Wilson Birthplace and Museum.

Farther down I-81 in Lexington is Virginia Military Institute (VMI), the nation's first state-supported military college. Key campus attractions include the VMI Museum (see Chapter 35), the George C. Marshall Museum, and the Corps of Cadets dress parade staged most Friday afternoons.

On an adjacent Lexington campus is Washington and Lee University, founded in 1749 and later endowed by George Washington. Robert E. Lee served as president of the school during the last five years of his life. In the Lee Chapel and Museum, visitors can visit Lee's preserved office and the famous statue portraying a sleeping–not dead, as many think–Lee on the field of battle, surrounded by tattered and worn Confederate flags captured during the Civil War.

Farther south in Roanoke, Hollins College hosts an annual literary festival that attracts noted writers from throughout the country. Hollins has become known for its writing programs.

A southern excursion to Ferrum leads to the Blue Ridge Institute and Farm Museum, the state's official folklore center, on the grounds of Ferrum College. Dedicated to the documentation and interpretation of traditional life and culture in the Virginia mountains, the institute offers various types of learning experiences, as well as a living-history farm museum.

To the southwest, in Blacksburg, visitors to Virginia Tech can tour a living museum of plant material in the

Horticulture Gardens. And in addition to wandering the gardens from sunrise to sunset, visitors can participate in many annual activities, including plant sales and give-aways. Weekenders at nearby Radford University can roam the Corinna de la Burde Sculpture Court, endowed by the late Roger de la Burde of Richmond. The sculpture garden is part of Radford's Flossie Martin Gallery.

At Emory and Henry College, located farther down I-81, in Emory, travelers can enjoy a self-guided walking tour of the campus. In folksy anecdotes, the accompanying pamphlet explains the college's colorful history on the southwestern frontier during the 1800s.

Virginia's coal-mining country near the Kentucky border is home to the Clinch Valley College of the University of Virginia. Founded in 1954, the school is located on the former "poor farm" of Wise County. Two native-stone buildings, which once housed indigent county residents, still stand on the campus.

From small country campuses to modern technological wonders, Virginia's colleges can make ideal weekend destinations. They all get high marks from visitors.

Specifically: For further information, contact: Bridgewater College, 703-828-2501; Christopher Newport University, 804-594-7000; Clinch Valley College of the University of Virginia, 703-328-0100; Eastern Mennonite College and Seminary, 703-432-4211; Emory and Henry College, 703-944-4121; Ferrum College, 703-365-4416; Hampden-Sydney College, 804-223-6000; Hampton University, 804-727-5000; Hollins College, 703-362-6000; George Mason University, 703-993-8700; James Madison University, 703-568-3356; Longwood College, 804-395-2001; Mary Baldwin College, 804-887-7031; Mary Washington College, 703-899-4681;

Norfolk State University, 804-623-8600; Old Dominion University, 804-683-3159; Radford University, 703-831-5324; Randolph-Macon Woman's College, 804-846-7392; Sweet Briar College, 804-381-6100; Union Theological Seminary, 804-355-0671; University of Virginia, 804-924-0311; Virginia Commonwealth University, 804-367-0100; Virginia Military Institute, 703-464-7000; Virginia Tech, 703-231-6000; Virginia State University, 804-524-5000; Washington and Lee University, 704-463-8400; and the College of William and Mary, 804-221-4000.

35 Visiting the VMI Museum
Lexington

This is not some stuffy and boring museum. The Virginia Military Institute Museum presents the glorious past and exciting present of the nation's oldest state-supported military college. It is worth a weekend trip for individuals and families intrigued by Virginia's college traditions (see Chapter 34) and VMI's unique history.

Located in the beautiful college town of Lexington (see Chapter 29), VMI has a long and strong heritage of producing citizen-soldiers. It was founded on November 11, 1839, when Maj. Gen. Francis H. Smith, a distinguished graduate of West Point, was named the first superintendent.

Among the early faculty members was Thomas "Stonewall" Jackson, professor of natural philosophy from 1851 until he left for the Civil War in 1861. Other distinguished professors included Matthew Fontaine Maury, whose work in charting the ocean currents had earned him the title "Pathfinder of the Seas," and John Mercer Brooke, the designer of the armor for the Confederate ironclad ship, the *Merrimac*.

Many VMI men have been successful in military and civilian life. On May 15, 1864, the VMI Corps of Cadets engaged Union forces in the Battle of New Market. Ten cadets were killed and forty-seven wounded, marking the only time in American history that an entire college's student body fought in a pitched battle as a single unit.

VMI's most famous graduate was George C. Marshall. After graduating in 1901, Marshall went on to attain the highest military rank possible – General of the Army. He later became Secretary of State and was the only professional soldier ever to be awarded the Nobel Prize for Peace, thanks to the European recovery program he devised known as "The Marshall Plan."

This honorable tradition can all be explored under one roof at the VMI Museum. It is located on VMI's campus in the basement of Jackson Memorial Hall, which also has on view a giant painting depicting the Battle of New Market.

The museum is packed with history. A tour begins with a fascinating review of the school's development, including many interesting artifacts from the early days, a re-creation of Superintendent Francis H. Smith's office, and class rings through the years (VMI graduates wear some of the largest class rings in the nation).

Next on the tour are exhibits depicting typical cadet barracks life and the uniforms worn at VMI. Life at VMI is disciplined and spartan, and the displays provide an inside look at what it's like to be a cadet there. VMI alumni often come to view this exhibit and to remember their own days in the barracks.

The Hall of Valor pays tribute to the many military accomplishments and acts of heroism in which VMI graduates have participated. Hundreds of medals and decorations for valor, as well as six Medals of Honor, attest to their courage. This quiet room is awe-inspiring to most visitors.

An impressive display about Stonewall Jackson is the next tour highlight. It includes the uniform he wore as a professor at VMI and the bullet-pierced raincoat he wore at Chancellorsville. Nearby is a mounted display of Little Sorrel, Jackson's war horse.

The rest of VMI is also enjoyable to explore. Cadets are available at VMI's Leujeune Hall to conduct free guided tours of the post. It makes for a great way to spend part of a weekend in Lexington.

Specifically: The hours of the VMI Museum (703-464-7232) are 9:00 A.M. to 5:00 P.M. Monday to Saturday and

2:00 P.M. to 5:00 P.M. on Sunday. There is no admission charge.

For further information about the Lexington area and a wide variety of quaint weekend accommodation options, contact the Lexington Visitors Bureau and visitors center at 102 East Washington Street, Lexington, VA 24450, 703-463-3777.

36 Northern Virginia's Lansdowne Resort
Leesburg

Within 100 miles of Washington, D.C., there are dozens of excellent hotels, hundreds of places to spend the weekend, and thousands of great restaurants. But there is only one place you can go that combines the service and attention to detail of a luxury hotel, a complete range of recreational options, a full-service spa and salon, and an award-winning golf course. That one place is Lansdowne Resort.

Located just ten miles from Washington's Dulles International Airport on a gorgeous 200-acre bluff overlooking the Potomac River, Lansdowne has captured several major awards in the hospitality industry. It has become a weekend wonderland for northern Virginians and other Washington, D.C.–area residents.

The eighteen-hole championship golf course, a signature layout created by world-renowned course designer Robert Trent Jones Jr., has received many golf industry awards. The resort also boasts an Executive Fitness Center with circuit training, aerobic workout equipment, indoor and outdoor pools, three whirlpool spas, a steam room and sauna, and a complete racquet sports program.

In addition to the recreation program, Lansdowne offers a full menu of spa services, including massage therapy, skin treatments, and hair care, all designed to pamper weekend guests with the utmost in personal luxury. These extras make it an ideal place for the golf widow (or widower) to head to when their hackers are on the links.

Families are also welcome. Lansdowne features its "Resort Rascals" supervised children's program every weekend. Kids aged three to twelve participate in golf and tennis clinics, arts and crafts, nature hikes, and other exciting activities, while their parents are free to enjoy a few hours of "adult time."

Lansdowne is home to two full-service restaurants, an outdoor cafe, and a tavern. Riverside Hearth, with its soaring windows and expansive views of Sugarloaf Mountain and the surrounding countryside, serves freshly prepared regional American cuisine. Potomac Grille offers a decidedly meat-and-potatoes attitude and a warm club-like atmosphere. Fairways, over at the golf course, serves light fare at a casual tee-side setting or outdoors, beside the pool. Stonewall's, the lobby-side tavern, is highlighted by a massive fieldstone fireplace.

The accommodations round out a perfect resort weekend destination. Rich fabrics and wall coverings, polished woods, and lavish amenities provide a relaxing atmosphere for you to enjoy when you aren't enjoying the rest of Lansdowne's resort life.

Specifically: Contact Lansdowne Resort at 44050 Wood-bridge Parkway, Leesburg, VA 22075, 703-729-8400 or 800-541-4801.

37 On Top of the World at Mountain Lake

If you want to feel at the top of the fall world, head to Mountain Lake, near Pembroke. This historic mountain resort features 2,600 acres of tall trees, stunning mountain scenery, and a clear mountain lake. It's a refreshing way to spend a fall weekend in the mountains.

Fed by underground streams, Mountain Lake is one of few natural freshwater lakes in the state. The location has served as a resort destination since 1857 and the massive native-stone hotel has overlooked the lake since 1936. Mountain Lake was developed into a legendary resort by William Lewis Moody and his daughter Mary Moody Northen. It was the site selected for filming the movie *Dirty Dancing* in fall 1986.

Accommodation options include hotel rooms and suites, as well as the rustic Chestnut Lodge nestled in the trees. Fireplaces and whirlpool baths are featured in some rooms. In warm months, unique cottages are also available.

The hotel offers great stone fireplaces on crisp days and filling meals in the rustically elegant dining room. There are spectacular views of the lake from the hotel, as the reds and golds of the trees add a warm glow.

Activities at Mountain Lake include hiking on trails all around the lake and surrounding mountains, boating, carriage rides, nature programs, and much more. It's a wonderfully serene atmosphere in which to pursue as much (or as little) as you want in the great outdoors or indoors.

Fall also means Oktoberfest at Mountain Lake. This annual event has become big business (and fun) at the resort and has filled the fall weekends with toasting, feasting, and music. It makes for another colorful part of a weekend at the top of the world.

Specifically: Contact Mountain Lake at Mountain Lake, VA 24136, 703-626-7121 or 800-346-3334.

38 Peaks of Otter
Bedford

Peaks of Otter brings a peak experience to fall visitors. This 4,200-acre resort is nestled in a valley amidst three mountains that make up Peaks of Otter – Sharp Top, Flat Top, and Harkening Hill.

Situated in a quiet lakeside setting just off the Blue Ridge Parkway, the Peaks of Otter offers a rustic decor of natural woods and subtle colors, with standard hotel rooms that all feature two double beds, private baths, and secluded balconies or terraces with wonderful views of Abbot Lake. But with so much to see and do, most guests spend little time in their rooms.

The best way to experience Peaks of Otter is on foot. The nearby visitors center offers advice and trail maps, a listing of activities, and exhibits on local history and native flora and fauna.

Some favorite fall trails include: Sharp Top, Harkening Hill Loop, Elk Run Loop, James River Locks, and Flat Top. They vary widely in length and difficulty.

After a hike, the hotel's famous food is the first priority. Big breakfasts and lunches are available for hungry hikers, but it's the dinners that draw guests from throughout the region. During the week (and on Saturday nights), the menu features a wide array of continental and local cuisine, with rainbow trout, ribs, and country ham among the favorites. On Friday nights, the restaurant offers a mountain of fresh seafood at the popular Friday seafood buffet. On Sundays, you can choose from the Sunday breakfast buffet or the Sunday country buffet, offering the best of southern cooking.

From hiking to hunger, Peaks of Otter provides the

answer. It's a great place to spend a fall weekend, as well as any other weekend in the mountains year-round.

Specifically: Contact Peaks of Otter at P.O. Box 489, Bedford, VA 24523, 703-586-1081 or 800-542-5927 (only in Virginia).

39 Weekends with a Spiritual Side

Whatever a person's religion or beliefs, there is no more appropriate place to begin a search for spiritual sanctuary than Virginia, birthplace of religious freedom in America.

During the mid-eighteenth century, many reformers and activists rebelled against the oppression of the Church of England and settled in the Commonwealth to petition for change. Their individual acts of courage changed the climate of intolerance and laid the groundwork for the nation's first statute of religious freedom, authored by Thomas Jefferson in 1785 and presented by James Madison. It found its way into Virginia's Bill of Rights and the First Amendment of the Constitution.

Start a spiritual journey in the state's capital of Richmond at St. John's Church, the site of Patrick Henry's famous "liberty or death" speech. Tours of the church are available daily and reenactments of the speech are held on summer Sundays and at other special times during the year.

An ever-growing collection of local Jewish history can be found at Congregation Beth Ahabah Museum and Archives Trust on Franklin Street. Established in 1789, the congregation – one of the oldest in America – has a rich heritage in Richmond that can be traced to Revolutionary hero and Jewish settler Jacob I. Cohen.

The Chesterfield County Courthouse Complex, about sixteen miles from Richmond, provides another glimpse of the area's religious history. A monument on the grounds and a painting of "The Apostles of Religious Freedom" at the Chesterfield County Museum honor seven men who were jailed there in the 1700s for practicing the Baptist faith in defiance of the established Anglican Church.

Farther south, in Petersburg, you'll find two historic

*St. John's Church, Richmond, where Patrick Henry gave his
famous "Give me liberty or give me death" speech*

African-American churches. The First Baptist Church on Harrison Street is believed to be the oldest Black church in America. Although the original church building was constructed in 1774, the current building dates from 1870. Nearby, Gillfield Baptist Church is the second-oldest Black church in America, dating back to 1786.

Over in Colonial Williamsburg (see Chapter 15), the restored eighteenth-century town offers fascinating tours of Bruton Parish church. It was a key social and religious center for the colonists.

Downtown Norfolk (see Chapter 22) is home to two attractions with both religious and historical significance. The Moses Myers townhouse, built in 1792 by the first Jewish family to live in Norfolk, is the only historic house in the nation to feature information on Jewish practices during Colonial times. St. Paul's Episcopal Church, just a block away, was built in 1739 and is Norfolk's only building that survived bombardment by the British in 1776.

In Virginia Beach, thousands of visitors of all spiritual traditions come to the Association for Research and Enlightenment (see Chapter 21) to study and to attend programs concerning the spiritual and psychic history of Edgar Cayce and others. Cayce, the best-documented psychic of the twentieth century, founded his headquarters in Virginia Beach in 1931. The center offers guided tours and many interesting programs.

Farther inland, but still in Virginia Beach, is Pat Robertson's Christian Broadcasting Network, where the "700 Club" program is produced. Visitors can tour the studio and stay at the adjacent Founder's Inn (see Chapter 17). The four-diamond hotel and conference center has 249 rooms and suites, formal and informal dining, full athletic facilities, and much more. Alcohol and tobacco are only occasionally allowed. The environment is a favorite for many people who seek spiritual renewal.

Down in Bedford County, visitors may be surprised to find Holy Land USA, a reproduction of Israel's sacred way, created along a four-mile trail. During the walk or covered farm-wagon tour, travelers will see re-creations of the highlights of the Holy Land, including Calvary and Jesus' empty tomb.

In nearby Buckingham County, a 700-acre commune on the south bank of the James River is home to Indian guru Swami Satchidananda and his disciples. Its centerpiece is the Light of Truth Universal Shrine, dedicated to bringing together all beliefs in the interest of world peace. Lodging and meals are available through the Lotus Inn at Yogaville, making for a unique spiritual weekend.

The spirit of George Washington lives on in the streets of Old Town Alexandria (see Chapter 49). Visitors to Christ Church can see the white box pew once owned by Washington, who was a parish vestryman there in 1765.

Specifically: For further information, contact: St. John's Church, 804-648-5015; Congregation Beth Ahabah Museum and Archives Trust, 804-353-2668; Chesterfield County Courthouse Complex and Chesterfield County Museum, 804-748-1026; First Baptist Church, 804-732-2841; Gillfield Baptist Church, 804-733-2404; Bruton Parish, 804-220-7645 or 800-HISTORY; Moses Myer House, 804-627-2737; Association for Research and Enlightenment, 804-428-3588; Christian Broadcasting Network and Founder's Inn, 804-523-7123 or 800-926-4466 (reservations); Holy Land USA, 703-586-2823; Light of Truth Universal Shrine and Lotus Inn, 804-969-4052 or 804-969-4801 (reservations); and Christ Church, 703-549-1450.

Winter

40 Hit the Slopes

A skiing weekend at one of the Old Dominion's ski resorts is sure to be a highlight of any winter season.

Virginia ski resorts excel in everything from discounted packages, elaborate sports complexes, and lavish pools and spas to year-round hiking trails and golf courses. They provide the makings for a first-rate weekend experience.

The key to enjoying a weekend on and off the ski slopes is choosing the resort that best suits your needs. Massanutten, Bryce, and Wintergreen (see Chapter 2) are all planned communities with year-round recreational options such as golf, swimming, racquetball, tennis, and hiking. Each resort has top-notch townhouses, condominiums, and private homes, but each one has its own distinct personality. The Homestead (see Chapter 45) ski area is very different, with a sedate, five-star resort setting and an all-Austrian ski school.

Bryce resort, only two hours from Washington, D.C., is located in the beautiful Shenandoah Valley, where the mountains rise to the West Virginia state line. Bryce is eleven miles west of the Mt. Jackson exit of I-81, so it's easy to reach by car. For fly-ins, Bryce has a 2,240-foot paved airstrip at the base of the ski slopes.

By concentrating on a superb ski school and racing

instruction, Bryce makes the most out of five separate runs, which fan out on a 500-vertical-foot mountainside. Bryce uses every bit of its trail network, wide bowl, and beginner area to create the expansive, open feeling of a small, western-style resort. It also recently added an additional slope and snowmaking equipment.

Surrounding the base complex and runs are 3,000 acres of woodlands containing 2,500 building lots. Nearly 1,000 private chalets, condominiums, and townhouses are either slopeside or near the lifts.

There is a very strong family side to Bryce, including the SkiWee Children's School for kids ages four to seven. A popular feature of the skiing is a large beginner area outside the base lodge. Inside the lodge, a dining room, lounge, fireplace with a crackling fire, and the flag-draped cathedral ceilings create an inviting and festive atmosphere for dinner, drinks in the lounge, or popular hearty Sunday buffets.

The Homestead has earned the prestigious Five-Star Award for more than thirty consecutive years. The resort's slopes are divided equally among beginner, intermediate, and advanced.

A one-mile shuttle from the grand hotel, the slopes are ideal for beginners and other skiers looking to become accomplished parallel skiers. Most of the 700-foot vertical drop is covered in several wide turns off the top.

The Homestead hosts the Sepp Kober Ski School that recruits a dozen European instructors each year. Kober, an Austrian known as the "father of southern skiing," has directed ski schools in Austria, Spain, and Norway and coached for the Spanish and Norwegian ski federations.

Overnight winter guests at The Homestead can savor excellent accommodations, elegant dining, a full-service spa, and the finest surroundings at attractively discounted package rates. The resort features 600 beautifully appointed rooms and a gracious staff that exudes southern hospitality.

Alternatives to the luxurious accommodations at The Homestead are Hot Springs and nearby Warm Springs – both replete with charming and moderately priced country inns nestled in beautiful mountain surroundings.

Located just twelve miles from the Harrisonburg exit off I-81, Massanutten boasts the best vertical slope to be found in all of Virginia, Maryland, and Pennsylvania at 1,110 vertical feet. With all fourteen slopes now under lights, the resort offers some of the best night skiing in the area.

The old favorites at Massanutten are 2,800-foot intermediate Rebel Yell and its more difficult sister, Dixie Dare. They're challenging if you want to push yourself, but you don't have to be a world champ to enjoy them. The two newest runs, expert Diamond Jim and intermediate ParaDice, are both more than 3,000 feet long and are served by a 2,100-foot quad lift that moves lines quickly.

Mountain lodging is available through the resort rental office, offering access to Le Club, a $3.2 million sports complex, with racquetball, basketball, volleyball, an Olympic-sized pool, a well-equipped exercise room, hot tubs, and sauna. Nearby hotels in Harrisonburg offer cost-saving "stay and ski" packages.

Wintergreen Resort, a popular four-season resort, nestled near the Blue Ridge Parkway about forty-five minutes from Charlottesville, was selected by *Better Homes and Gardens* and *Family Circle* as one of the top family resorts in the country. It's definitely true for skiing families hitting the slopes on the weekend.

Wintergreen has built a superb reputation as a premier

eastern resort destination, based on luxurious condominium lodging, a sports complex, an award-winning ski patrol, children's programs, plenty of great restaurants, and one of the longest ski runs in the south.

Wintergreen was designed with both skiers and non-skiers in mind. Well-groomed slopes are guaranteed to get beginners off to a good start, while a separate and highly demanding trail system is reserved for advanced skiers only. The five advanced trails, call "The Highlands," cover more than 1,000 vertical feet. A total of seventeen slopes and trails serve the resort.

The 36,000-square-foot Skyline Pavilion is a modern $3.5 million skier services building with everything under one roof. Within a short walk of two village centers – with pools, restaurants, shops, banquet and meeting rooms – are more than 400 fully appointed condominiums and the Trillium House Country Inn, a popular twelve-room bed and breakfast with lots of Blue Ridge charm.

Specifically: Contact Bryce Resort at P.O. Box 3, Basye, VA 22810, 703-856-2121. Contact The Homestead at P.O. Box 1000, Hot Springs, VA 24445, 703-839-5500. Contact Massanutten at P.O. Box 1227, Harrisonburg, VA 22801, 703-289-9441. Contact Wintergreen at Wintergreen Resort, Wintergreen, VA 22958, 804-325-2200.

41 Weekend Fun in Fredericksburg

Many I-95 weekend drivers don't know that the history haven of Fredericksburg is just off the interstate. They don't have to drive any farther for a historic weekend.

Fredericksburg is great for weekend walking and driving because there's so much to see in a small space. Head straight for the modern visitors center at 706 Caroline Street, where the staff can provide a map and specific touring, dining, and overnight recommendations.

In the city center, the first stop is the Hugh Mercer Apothecary Shop at 1020 Caroline Street, named for Dr. Mercer, who practiced medicine and ran the pharmacy. Opened in 1771, it is one of the oldest apothecary shops in the nation. The shop has been restored to its eighteenth-century appearance, with lots of medicine bottles, pills, and prescriptions.

The Rising Sun Tavern at 1306 Caroline Street was the social and political center of early life in Fredericksburg. It was built by George Washington's youngest brother, Charles, in 1760 and played host to most of the key colonial patriots. The restored building now features the Tap Room bar and the gentlemen's chambers, where four men typically spent the night in one small bed.

The James Monroe Law Office and Museum at 908 Charles Street is where Monroe began his successful private and public career. Eventually Monroe held more high offices than any other president. Though there's lots of Monroe memorabilia, the most interesting item is a Louis XVI desk, which was used for the signing of the Monroe Doctrine.

The Mary Washington House at 1200 Charles Street was purchased by George for his mother. Many of Mrs. Washington's belongings remain, and a beautiful English garden has been maintained in the back (look for her sundial and the boxwood she planted long ago). Her peaceful gravesite and monument are on Washington Avenue at the end of Pitt Street.

Kenmore, at 1201 Washington Avenue, was the elegant eighteenth-century plantation home of George Washington's only sister, Betty. During a guided tour, visitors can see a giant diorama of Fredericksburg as it was in 1765 and many Washington family artifacts that offer much insight into plantation life.

One highlight of a Fredericksburg visit is a tour of the A. Smith Bowman Distillery. This legendary company makes Virginia Gentleman, "the whiskey of Virginia." A tour of its beautifully renovated buildings is interesting and educational, but call ahead to make sure a Virginia gentleman or gentlewoman is available to provide you with a taste of Virginia.

You should spend at least one night in Fredericksburg, and there are lots of lodging and dining options in the area. In keeping with the historic theme, try the Fredericksburg Colonial Inn at 1707 Princess Anne Street. This thirty-room Civil War–era inn is located right in the historic district.

For a great period meal (as well as nice accommodations), head for the Kenmore Inn at 1200 Princess Anne Street. A romantic and historic inn, it also offers a restaurant and a pub. You should also allow time to shop at the Made in Virginia Shop at 807 Caroline Street. It's the perfect place for a gift that could only come from the Old Dominion.

Specifically: Contact the Fredericksburg visitors center at 804-373-1776 or 800-678-4748; A. Smith Bowman Distillery, 703-373-4555; Fredericksburg Colonial Inn at 804-371-5666; Kenmore Inn of Fredericksburg at 804-371-7622; and the Made in Virginia Shop at 804-371-2030 or 800-635-3149.

42 The Boar's Head Inn & Sports Club
Charlottesville

The Boar's Head Inn, with the ambiance of a Virginia country estate, sprawls on fifty-three acres in the genteel Charlottesville countryside. In this pristine setting, surrounded by manicured horse farms and by the burgeoning Monticello wine district (see Chapter 32), the Boar's Head Inn continues to charm and relax weekend guests as it has done for nearly three decades.

More than one and a half centuries after Thomas Jefferson's time, the inn proves that one can still experience the Virginia hospitality for which Jefferson was renowned. Against the spectacular backdrop of the Blue Ridge Mountains, just a stone's throw from Jefferson's beloved Monticello (see Chapter 10), the Boar's Head Inn brings to life the delights of an old-fashioned weekend in the Virginia countryside.

But this resort is anything but old-fashioned when it comes to modern amenities. The inn offers 175 spacious rooms and suites with modern-day conveniences (and colonial-era furnishings and art), world-class tennis, a full-service sports club, pools, saunas, facials, massages, stunning hot-air ballooning, golf at the adjacent eighteen-hole championship Birdwood Golf course, and much more.

Dining at Boar's Head is (or should be) a highlight of any weekend stay. The historic Old Mill Room restaurant is one of only a handful in the Commonwealth to hold the Automobile Association of America's coveted Four Diamonds award. The unique nineteenth-century candlelight setting, the creative menu, and the award-winning wine list make an Old Mill

Room meal a very special occasion during a very special weekend stay.

Specifically: Contact the Boar's Head Inn & Sports Club at US 250 West, Charlottesville, VA 22901, 804-296-2181 or 800-476-1988.

43 Middleburg

Middleburg is one of Virginia's many ideal winter weekend destinations. It's hard to believe there is so much beautiful countryside so close to the urban craziness of Washington, D.C. But Middleburg and the surrounding area provide the perfect country weekend experience for D.C.-dwellers and others in the area.

The town of Middleburg was established (purchased for $2.50 an acre) in 1787 by Virginia statesman and Revolutionary War Lt. Col. Leven Powell. It was originally called Chinn's Crossroads, after Joseph Chinn, a first cousin of George Washington's. Powell changed the name to Middleburg because of the town's location between Alexandria and Winchester along the Ashby Gap Road (now US 50).

Middleburg has welcomed travelers for more than 250 years, serving as a staging and resting point for early country road "drivers." Today, Middleburg still welcomes travelers with open arms. The historic town offers many excellent restaurants, shops, and places to stay. The sidewalks are typically crowded with visitors exploring the quaint town on foot.

Middleburg welcomes guests looking for small town charm, good wine from local vineyards, and the fox hunting and horse scene. The town has a classy air to it and is in a class of its own.

The cute little Pink Box visitors center, at 12 North Madison Street, can help with sightseeing, shopping, dining, and accommodation options. There's usually a friendly local woman there with a charming southern accent and a love of the Middleburg area.

The Red Fox Inn and Tavern is a great place to begin your exploration of Middleburg. It is billed as the "oldest original inn in America" and served both as the meeting spot for Confederate Col. John Mosby and his Rangers and as a press conference spot for President Kennedy's press secretary Pierre Salinger. It now serves up great food, cold drink, and wonderful rooms for those who can spend the night (and everyone should).

Among the many great places to stay and eat in Middleburg are: the Middleburg Country Inn, the Middleburg Inn & Guest Suites, Mosby's Tavern for hearty fare, and the Upper Crust for sweets.

Across the street (US 50) from the Red Fox is the Windsor House Inn. It was known as the Colonial Inn during the Civil War and was run by Catherine Broun. Though a Confederate sympathizer, she served generous meals to Union troops at the inn when they occupied the town in 1862.

Along with sleeping and eating, you'll want to investigate some other options in Middleburg, such as: its super shopping, visiting a nearby vineyard (see list below), or simply driving through the rolling horse and hunt country. What a great way to spend a weekend!

Specifically: Contact the Pink Box visitors center at 703-687-8888; the Red Fox Inn and Tavern, 703-687-6301; Middleburg Country Inn, 703-687-6082; Middleburg Inn & Guest Suites, 703-587-3115 or 800-432-6125; Mosby's Tavern, 703-687-5282; Upper Crust, 703-687-5666; and the Windsor House Inn, Middleburg, 703-777-5000.

Local vineyards include Swedenburg Estate Vineyard, 703-687-5219; Piedmont Vineyards, Middleburg, 703-687-5528; and Meredyth Vineyards, Middleburg, 703-687-6277.

44 Martha Washington Inn
Abingdon

> If you want to find a true school,
> Come to Martha;
> Housed within a mansion old
> Where traditions oft are told
> Of the soldier lovers bold;
> Up at Martha.
>
> — old soldier's song about the
> Martha Washington Inn

The Martha Washington Inn is a nugget of gold in the mine of weekend opportunities in southwest Virginia. This elegant old hotel serves as the perfect base for exploring Abingdon and the rest of southwest Virginia (see Chapter 30).

The Martha, as it's affectionately called, was originally built in 1832 as a large southern mansion by Gen. Francis Preston and his family of nine. An $8 million renovation has made this an elegantly hospitable southwest Virginia retreat.

Situated right on Main Street, the hotel features 500-plus antiques, four-poster canopied beds, and many majestic reminders of the past, as well as the modern amenities of a luxury hotel. The rooms, the service, and the dining are well worth the trip to this far corner of Virginia and serve as a haven at the end of a long drive. Ask some of the older staff members about the Martha's unique history, including: the hotel's stint as a girl's school; the legend of the riderless Yankee horse; a Civil War soldier loved and protected by a local schoolgirl, but ultimately slain; and illustrious visitors such as Eleanor Roosevelt, Harry Truman, Lady Bird Johnson, Jimmy Carter, and Elizabeth Taylor.

The rest of the town of Abingdon is also packed with history, historic homes, and quaint shops. A walk along Main

Street is a pleasant way to spend a few hours and it's just outside the front entrance of the Martha.

The first stop should be the Barter Theatre. This historic playhouse evolved when Robert Porterfield brought a troupe of unemployed actors together in 1933. They exchanged theater tickets for produce, livestock, and other goods brought by local people and a legend was born. Today, the Barter Theatre is the State Theatre of Virginia. For an enjoyable evening, try to catch a performance between the spring and fall.

To help you continue your Main Street exploration, you might want to pick up a walking tour brochure. It can advise you on planning your walk and tell you more about the buildings, many of which have excellent explanatory markers. The William King House, the Washington County Courthouse, and Dunn's Hotel/Virginia House are particularly interesting and photogenic.

It's an easy walk back to the Martha and a night of rest and relaxation. This nugget is definitely worth its weight in gold.

Specifically: Contact the Martha Washington Inn at 150 West Main Street, Abingdon, VA 24210, 703-628-3161 or 800-533-1014. For further information about Abingdon, contact the Abingdon Convention and Visitors Bureau at 208 West Main Street, Abingdon, VA 24210, 703-676-2282 or 800-435-3440. For show information, contact the Barter Theatre at P.O. Box 867, Abingdon, VA 24210, 703-628-3991 or 800-368-3240.

45 The Homestead
Hot Springs

> "I remained here six days, and took the bath every day,
> with the best results."
> —Peregrine Prolix, 1837
> *Letters Descriptive of the Virginia Springs*

Historically (and in reality) The Homestead is one of Virginia's (and the nation's) finest resorts. A weekend spent here is truly one of the finest pleasures you'll find in the Old Dominion (and in life).

As you drive downhill and into town, The Homestead unfolds before you like a rich oriental carpet. This sprawling property is a southern-style resort steeped in tradition dating back to 1766, but with many modern travel touches. You enter another world when you pull up to the elegant entrance and allow the crisply efficient staff to take care of your car and luggage. Leave your worries in your auto.

For more than 225 years, people have come to The Homestead to restore and refresh themselves in the invigorating mountain air and the soothing, healing, hot spring waters. In years past, it was thought that the waters could cure or relieve the symptoms of ailments such as gout, rheumatism, arthritis, neuritis, lumbago, hypertension, nephritis, and nervous disorders. Today, many still find their troubles melt away at this relaxing spa.

Legend and local history say that The Homestead's hot springs were discovered by an Indian brave traveling through the mountains in the sixteenth century. He evidently found a spring of warm water, drank from it, slept, awoke the next day invigorated, and then spread the tale of his discovery.

Dr. Thomas Walker, who explored the valley in 1750, wrote, "We went to Hot Springs . . . the spring is clear and warmer than new milk and there is a spring of cold water within twenty feet of the warm one." In 1755, George Washington visited Hot Springs while on an inspection tour of forts along the Allegheny frontier. Many travelers followed, and The Homestead was opened and grew to accommodate them.

Check-in is just off the Great Hall, with its plush furnishings, many fireplaces, and lounging guests. It's always enjoyable to be led to your room in anticipation of the luxuries that await.

Homestead rooms are unique and more like those of a small country inn. There's so much to see and do, however, that you rarely spend too much time in your room.

A weekend is not nearly long enough to enjoy all that The Homestead has to offer. There are so many pleasurable pursuits indoors and outdoors that it's just a matter of pursuing your passion.

Here's a short list of favorite Homestead activities: shopping along Cottage Row; fishing in a mountain stream; skeet shooting; bowling; tennis in a beautiful setting; horseback riding; hiking; and skiing in the winter.

Golf is a big draw for many guests. There are three courses nestled in the Allegheny Mountains. The Homestead Course features a first tee, originally built in 1892, which remains the oldest tee in continuous use in the U.S.

The Spa, another popular spot, is legendary for the restorative powers of its hot springs. Built in 1892, The Spa is one of the first European-style spas and bathhouses in the country.

You can just relax in the indoor or outdoor pools or you can go for the full treatment. The facility features a full-service hydrotherapeutic center offering various baths, steam-room sauna, salt glow, Swiss shower, Scotch spray, massage, and much more. It's the ultimate way to remove any weekday worries.

Once you feel fit, it's time for a filling meal. The Dining Room features a grand old gourmet experience with six-course classic menus, buffets, live entertainment, and ball-room dancing made magic by a magnificent, sparkling chandelier. The Grille offers late-night dining in a casual atmosphere. Cafe Albert is a cozy coffee house great for pastries and light fare.

Another favorite place for meals at The Homestead is Sam Snead's Tavern, a converted bank where Virginia wines are stored in the antique walk-in vault. The casual atmosphere and menu make for a nice lunch or dinner. American favorites include New York strip steak, fresh Virginia Allegheny Mountain rainbow trout, and the Tavern's hickory-smoked barbecued spareribs (a messy and tasty treat).

The Homestead offers many great special weekend rates and packages. A recent renovation means an even better weekend awaits guests.

Specifically: Contact The Homestead at US 220, Hot Springs, VA 24445, 703-839-5500 or 800-336-5771 (800-542-5734 in Virginia).

46 To B&B or Not to B&B, That Is Not the Question

Virginia is the perfect place to find a bed-and-breakfast or country inn for the weekend, and the Virginia Division of Tourism and Bed-and-Breakfast Association of Virginia have made it easy. By calling two numbers, you can receive enough information to make planning any bed-and-breakfast or inn weekend easy.

From elegant townhouses in northern Virginia's cosmopolitan communities to colonial homes overlooking the Chesapeake Bay to cabins tucked away in the Blue Ridge Mountains, Virginia's bed-and-breakfasts and country inns offer weekend guests the opportunity to enjoy gracious hospitality.

Lavish restorations of eighteenth- and nineteenth-century mansions beckon travelers to enjoy the quiet gentility of early-American life. Inns serving southern regional cuisine often complement dinners with wine from nearby vineyards. Quaint cottages and cozy cabins equipped with romantic fireplaces and quilted comforters offer the more casual atmosphere some visitors prefer.

From these accommodations, guests might enjoy a city walking tour or horseback riding in the country. They can shop for antiques or fish for tasty trout while staying in one of Virginia's hundreds of country inns and bed-and-breakfast establishments.

Specifically: Contact Virginia's toll-free bed-and-breakfast information line at 800-BNB-1293. Contact the B&B Association of Virginia at 703-672-0870.

47 Gold Leaf Inn
Danville

Danville is a true southern Virginia gem situated in the beautiful foothills region near the North Carolina border. Famed for its Millionaires Row of homes built by tobacco barons in the nineteenth century, the town – and the Gold Leaf Inn – are just made for quiet weekends.

The Gold Leaf Inn is a large Queen Anne–Victorian home built in 1897 with tobacco money and is located at the upper end of Millionaires Row. Pam and Jimmy Barbour are the third owners, and they have embarked on an ambitious renovation project for their guests. They've appropriately adopted tobacco leaves as their logo.

The house has been lovingly restored to combine the elegance of the old with modern conveniences. It features sunny porches, gardens, gazebos, and some of the area's best architecture.

The guest rooms offer an interesting mixture of antiques and modern furnishings, while the bathrooms (one is shared) feature antique tubs, showers, and a variety of amenities. The options for rooms include: the Virginia Spencer room (a sun-filled room with wicker furniture); the Mary Dodson room (a bright room with an antique wardrobe that fills one wall); and the William Whitfield room (historic Tibaut wallpaper and a private bath are the highlights of this romantic hideaway).

Breakfast might include homemade breads and muffins, cinnamon pecan pancakes, or an omelet with special spices and fillings. You won't depart hungry, but you will definitely depart with a different view of tobacco leaves.

Early winter is an ideal time to visit Danville and the Gold Leaf Inn. The tobacco auctions run through November, when you'll enjoy hearing and seeing the tobacco auctioneer's rhythmic chanting. But any winter weekend brings a warm welcome from the Gold Leaf Inn and the rest of the town. Danville features many historic houses, the Dan River Linen and Clothing Outlet, and the Museum of Fine Arts and History in the Sutherlin Mansion (the house known for its Civil War role as "The Last Capitol of the Confederacy").

Specifically: Contact the Gold Leaf Inn at 1012 Main Street, Danville, VA 24541, 804-793-1433.

48 The Lindow Row Inn
Richmond

Virginia has many beautifully big and luxurious hotels. The Homestead (see Chapter 45) and the Jefferson Hotel (see Chapter 50) come to mind. The Old Dominion also abounds in bed-and-breakfasts (see Chapter 46), each with its own charm and personality.

But for the best of both worlds, there's Richmond's Linden Row Inn, a medium-sized luxurious hotel, with all of the personal touches of a bed-and-breakfast. In 1988, this fascinating row of connected houses was lovingly augmented, restored, and given a new life as the seventy-three-room Linden Row Inn. It has now become a Richmond landmark in both the historic and modern sense.

The block the Linden Row Inn presides over was originally the site of an elegant garden known for its beautiful roses, jasmine, and lindens (providing the name to come later). It was in these gardens that Edgar Allan Poe played as a child, giving him the inspiration and setting for the enchanted garden in his love poem, "To Helen."

Ten houses were built between 1839 and 1853, and the structures were used as residences and a variety of girls' schools well into the twentieth century. In 1922, two of the original buildings were razed to make room for a medical arts building.

Now, the Linden Row Inn has become a unique and popular place to meet, dine, and stay. It is the perfect combination of a hotel and bed-and-breakfast, because guests receive the personal attention of a bed and breakfast, along with the amenities and services of a large hotel. Check-in is low-key, as is the evening wine-and-cheese reception (and on-going bar service) in the quiet parlor.

The connected buildings are situated around a large courtyard and provide a wide variety of rooms overlooking the pretty brick-walled gardens, patio, and streets. It's a true lodging haven for those tired of cookie-cutter hotels.

There are original fireplaces, marble mantels, and chandeliers throughout. A superb collection of gasoliers, pier mirrors, and mantel mirrors specifically assembled for Linden Row, accent the seven double-parlor suites and some of the stair halls.

Most of the rooms are situated in the four floors of the original row houses. They are entered from the wide porch at the back of the property, providing the residential feel that pervades the Linden Row Inn. Other unique rooms overlook the garden courtyard and patio, completing the sense of a small bed and breakfast that just happens to have many more rooms than most.

The Linden Row Inn's restaurant is quickly becoming a culinary favorite for locals as well as guests. The setting is fitting for a fine meal, with a small and subdued dining room just off the lobby and the courtyard.

Chef Alain Vincey, formerly the owner and chef at Richmond's famed La Maisonette, is the main attraction in the dining room. He has brought Virginia fare, with European flair, to the Linden Row Inn.

The ever-changing menu is a refreshing respite on the Richmond dining scene. Chef Vincey adds Virginia touches to many favorite dishes, providing unique versions of crab cakes, shrimp, fresh fish, ham, poultry, and beef. Each night may mean different interpretations of Old Dominion dishes.

A colorful continental (or full) breakfast in the dining room completes a stay at the Linden Row Inn. At check-out you'll feel you're saying good-bye to old friends and that you'll be back for a visit to their "house" soon.

Specifically: The Linden Row Inn is at 100 East Franklin Street, Richmond, VA 23219, 804-783-7000.

49 Old Town Alexandria

Old Town Alexandria is the quintessential Old Dominion old town. It's perfect for a historic winter weekend.

Old Town Alexandria was founded as a seaport way back in 1749. Known as George Washington's hometown, Alexandria is where Washington and fellow patriots attended the theater, church, and political meetings during the formative years of the Revolution.

Because of these historic beginnings and a massive preservation and restoration effort, Old Town Alexandria is a National Register of Historic Places National Landmark. It is filled with almost 1,000 preserved and restored eighteenth- and nineteenth-century buildings, which are now used as residences, businesses, restaurants, inns, and museums.

Among the historic landmarks and museums open to the public in Alexandria are the Ramsay House visitors center; the Lyceum (museum and exhibits); Gadsby's Tavern Museum; Fort Ward Museum (a large Civil War fort); the Black History Resource Center; Alexandria Archaeology; and the Torpedo Factory Art Center; all operated by the city's Office of Historic Alexandria.

Other historic attractions include: Christ Church (the eighteenth-century church attended by George Washington and Robert E. Lee); the Carlyle House (a typically lovely eighteenth-century mansion); the boyhood home of Robert E. Lee; the Lee-Fendall House (the 1785 mansion where Light Horse Harry Lee wrote the farewell address from Alexandrians to George Washington when he left Mount Vernon to become the first president); the Stabler-Leadbeater Apothecary Shop; and many other historic landmarks that make Alexandria a history-lover's mecca.

There's even more history within minutes of Alexandria.

*Both the Washingtons and the Lees worshipped
at Christ Church, Alexandria*

Washington's Mount Vernon, Woodlawn (built for Washington's foster daughter, Nelly Custis Lewis), and George Mason's Gunston Hall are all within minutes of your Old Town base.

All of this history means you need to spend at least one night in Old Town Alexandria. Some excellent options include: Morrison House (eighteenth-century-style manor house), Holiday Inn of Old Town, and the Executive Club (convenient apartment-style accommodations with full kitchens).

Old Town also offers a wide array of eclectic dining choices. Some long-time favorites include the Seaport Inn, the Fish Market, Gadsby's Tavern, and dozens of excellent ethnic options.

Specifically: The Ramsay House visitors center, at 221 King Street in the heart of Old Town, is open 9:00 A.M. to 5:00 P.M. daily except on Thanksgiving, Christmas, and New Year's Day. The friendly staff offers free twenty-four-hour passes for on-street, metered parking to out-of-town visitors, as well as museum tickets; gift items; and brochures for museums and attractions, restaurants, shopping, antique stores, accommodations, and special events. Arrangements for group tours may also be made at the Ramsay House. Contact the visitors center at 221 King Street, Alexandria, VA 22314-3209, 703-838-4200 or 800-388-9119.

For accommodation options, contact: Morrison House, 703-838-8000 or 800-367-0800; Holiday Inn of Old Town, 703-549-6080 or 800-368-5047; and the Executive Club, 703-739-2582 or 800-535-2582.

For dining options, contact: the Seaport Inn, 703-549-2341; the Fish Market, 703-836-5676; and Gadsby's Tavern, 703-548-1288.

50 The Jefferson Hotel
Richmond

The Jefferson Hotel is a perfect base for a weekend in Virginia's capital city of Richmond (see Chapter 1). The hotel has been the hub of Richmond social life since its opening back in 1895. Over the years, this elegant establishment has set the tone for fine accommodations and dining and has hosted nine presidents and a host of dignitaries, TV and film stars, and notables.

The hotel is located on Franklin Street, midway between Richmond's business and residential districts. It was totally restored, to the tune of $34 million, between 1983 and 1986 in order to recapture its former grandeur. But it took another renovation and many service upgrades for the Jefferson to finally receive Five Diamond status with the Automobile Association of America, awarded only to some fifty North American hotels each year.

Many items original to the hotel include ladies' writing tables, ornate wall sconces, and many oil paintings. It stands preserved as a fine example of Beaux Arts eclectic beauty.

There are two impressive lobbies at the Jefferson Hotel: the Palm Court and the Rotunda. The Palm Court is now the registration area and features the original bellman's desk and nine original stained-glass side windows. This area displays the marble statue of Thomas Jefferson, created for the hotel in the late 1800s by Richmond sculptor Edward V. Valentine. Live alligators lived in the pools beside the statue until 1948, but they have been replaced by cast-iron replicas. Afternoon tea is still served here.

The Rotunda is one of the most recognizable lobbies in the country, boasting faux-marble pillars supporting a seventy-foot ceiling that is embellished with multicolor and gold-leaf designs. The highlight of the room is the double-wide sweeping marble staircase, which many believe was the model for the famous stairway featured in "Gone With the Wind." Since the turn of the century, the Rotunda has hosted weekend guests including the Barrymore, Vanderbilt, and Whitney families, and such notable celebrities as Gertrude Stein, F. Scott and Zelda Fitzgerald, Charlie Chaplin, and Sarah Bernhardt.

The Jefferson's 274 luxurious guest rooms and suites feature fifty-seven delightfully different styles, all with unusually high ceilings, tall windows, and custom-designed and richly upholstered furnishings. From mahogany armoires to custom-woven carpets, you'll find a perfect weekend haven.

For a special weekend meal, visit the Jefferson's award-winning Lemaire restaurant. Named for Thomas Jefferson's maitre d', Lemaire features regional cuisine complemented by an extensive selection of fine Virginia wines. T. J.'s Grill and Bar overlooking the Rotunda provides a less formal atmosphere, where guests can enjoy lunch, dinner, or late-night fare.

The elegant setting, accommodations, and dining make for a perfect capital combination. The Jefferson Hotel provides a warm weekend welcome for winter or any other time of year.

Specifically: Contact the Jefferson Hotel at Franklin and Adams Streets, Richmond, VA 23220, 804-788-8000 or 800-424-8014.

51 Old-Time Mountain Music
Galax

Galax residents call their town the "World capital of old-time mountain music" and they mean it. A variety of activities, events, and sights make Galax a great place to spend a weekend with mountains and music.

Each winter, the Galax Downtown Association sponsors the Galax Mountain Music Jamboree. The performances feature old-time and bluegrass bands, as well as cloggers and other entertainers.

From October to May, the Jamboree is held the third Saturday of each month at the historic Rex Theatre on Grayson Street. The Rex is owned by the Galax Downtown Association and all proceeds go to the restoration of the theater.

An Old Fiddler's Convention and Fiddlefest are held the second weekend each August. The Jamboree is also held outside in June, July, and September, making Galax a four-season music mecca.

Be sure to stop by Barr's Fiddle Shop. Tom Barr, born into a musical family, grew up hearing old-time mountain music played by some of the best traditional musicians of the area. Barr's long-standing friendship with master fiddler and fiddlemaker Albert Hash piqued his interest in the making of fiddles. For more than twenty years, he has been creating the finest fiddles, banjos, dulcimers, and many other musical instruments. His shop is an old-time music marvel.

Other Galax highlights include: the Jeff Matthews Memorial Museum, with original Appalachian Mountain cabins; Rooftop of Virginia CAP Crafts, featuring locally made crafts; and the Blue Ridge Music Center, which is being developed by the National Park Service to preserve, interpret, and present traditional music of the Blue Ridge Mountains.

Galax is located in the midst of beautiful Blue Ridge

Fiddling around

mountain scenery. Only seven miles from the Blue Ridge Parkway (see Chapter 28), it is a trail head for the New River Trail State Park, Virginia's only linear park, which features excellent hiking, bicycling, and horseback riding.

Specifically: For further information about Galax's old-time mountain music, accommodations, dining, and shopping, contact the Galax Downtown Association at P.O. Box 544, Galax, VA 24333, 703-236-0668.

52 A Whale of a Weekend
Virginia Beach

A wintertime visit to Virginia Beach for whale watching is a unique adventure the whole family will enjoy. Special watching packages offered by many resort hotels can make this winter adventure a real money-saver.

The annual migration of the endangered humpback whales, among the world's largest mammals, can be viewed during a boat ride from the shores of Virginia Beach. Many of the juvenile whales are foregoing the annual Caribbean trek to enjoy the mild winters of Virginia Beach, taking advantage of the rich food sources available at the mouth of the Chesapeake Bay.

Boat trips are sponsored by the Virginia Marine Science Museum, Virginia's most-visited museum. Trips generally run from mid-January to mid-February, Fridays through Mondays. During the boat trips, it's possible to see the whales surfacing to breathe and to see them slap their tails as close as 100 yards away. (Whale sightings are not guaranteed and trips are subject to cancellation due to weather conditions.)

Whale-watching trips take place aboard sixty-five-foot headboats operated by experienced local captains. During each excursion, trained museum staff watch out for whales while they also conduct educational programs with props such as whale skeletal parts, teeth, and baleen pieces. In addition, visitors can often catch sight of birds rarely seen on land, such as the oceanic gannet. They also point out local landmarks, like the Old Cape Henry Lighthouse, the oldest government-built lighthouse in the country.

Specifically: For additional package information, contact the Virginia Beach visitor information center at 800-VA BEACH (822-3224). For additional information about specific whale-watching trips and the Virginia Marine Science Museum, call 804-437-4949.

Index